SMART
HORSE

SMART HORSE

Understanding the Science of
Natural Horsemanship

JENNIFER M. MacLEAY, DVM, PH.D.

ECLIPSE PRESS

Lexington, Kentucky

Library of Congress Control Number: 2003102041

ISBN 1-58150-099-8

Printed in the United States
First Edition: September 2003

Distributed to the trade by
National Book Network
4501 Forbes Boulevard
Suite 200
Lanham, MD 20706
1.800.462.6420

a division of
Blood-Horse Publications
PUBLISHERS SINCE 1916

ECLIPSE
PRESS

Contents

Introduction

This book is meant to be an introduction to the world of horse learning and cognition. If you can understand how horses learn and how they think, then you will be a better horse owner and trainer.

I am not a psychologist or animal behaviorist by training; I am a veterinarian and horse owner. I have found that the current trends in horse training through "natural" methods, without coercion or punishment, to be wonderful. These methods have contributed greatly to my life with horses both privately and professionally. However, as I explored these methodologies, I discovered the current horsemanship literature lacked some important explanations of how these methods are rooted in science and how they apply not only to horses, but to dogs, cats, dolphins, pigeons, and, even humans. I also discovered that many horse owners shared my confusion as to why certain training methods were "natural" and others not.

Therefore, my goal in writing this book is to be a translator, connecting the scientific literature to what you are being taught or are teaching in your daily lessons so that we may recognize there are fundamental principles of learning and training to which horses respond. My goal is to explain these principles in a way all horse owners can understand. You may then use that knowledge to make yourself a better horse trainer, owner, or educator.

Why is knowledge of animal behavior and cognition so important?

I began researching animal behavior and cognition because I wanted to understand how my teachers were communicating with my horses so that back home I could continue the work on my own. I am the type of person who needs to know the why and not just the how. And I suspect you are too; otherwise you would not have purchased this book. I was never content to see trainers teach in the round pen or in the arena and not want to know why the method they were using was better than another. By learning about animal behavior and cognition I have gained that insight. As you read this book, I hope that you will too.

Cognition is defined as the mental process by which knowledge is acquired and involves awareness, understanding, reasoning, judgment, intuition, and memory. If we understand how our horses think and learn, then we can understand why it is possible to teach a horse a particular behavior in different ways and have each way be successful. We can also understand why attempting to teach a behavior in a way that goes against how a horse naturally learns and understands may be unsuccessful.

I have applied the principles of learning and cognition that follow in this book to my relationship with my horses. This has allowed me to save time and money in their early training. However, as I do not consider myself to be a horse trainer, I have also found that understanding these principles has helped me be more reflective in my relationship with the professional horse trainers with whom I work.

By understanding how a horse may react in a particular situation you may be able to keep your horse quiet and under control in new or different situations, such as when the veterinarian comes to visit. Certainly from a professional point of view, learning techniques that are based on my understanding of how horses learn have allowed me to handle many poorly trained horses safely, making my daily work as a veterinarian easier.

Another point to keep in mind as you read this book is that horses, like people, are individuals. Even if you follow every principle outlined in this book, your horse will still have great days, good days, and days when he or she just doesn't want to perform. Remember this and understand when after two weeks of excellent progress your horse decides he's going to goof off a bit.

Introductions all around...

On the following pages I introduce two of the horses you will see in this book. They are Tieler (pronounced "tyler") and Reigna ("ray-na"). When I wrote the first version of this book, Tieler, a bay Thoroughbred gelding, was a three-year-old. Before the photos were taken, Tieler had experienced some round-pen training and a single saddling lesson.

Tieler is a full Thoroughbred and very brave. He did not inherit the nervous temperament of his dam or his half sister. However, he is a sensitive horse and works off of minimal pressure (compared to his sister). He also is a dominant horse and frequently challenges my authority. I did his early round-pen training myself.

Tieler's half sister is Reigna, five at the time of this writing. She is half-Thoroughbred and half-Oldenburg (her brand is ISR). She was started in a very traditional round

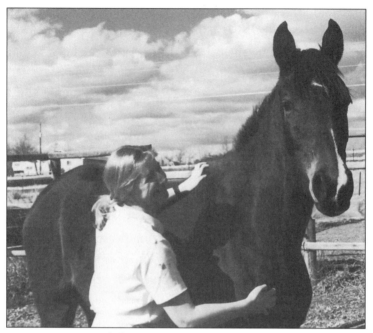

Tieler as a three-year-old.

pen/natural horsemanship style.

Her temperament is very similar to her Thoroughbred mother's; she is a worrier and frequently gets upset if you push her too quickly. Her Oldenburg side, though, makes her a much calmer horse than her mother. I started Reigna as a three-year-old with help from a trainer who practices natural horsemanship. Since that time I have worked with Reigna toward an ultimate goal of doing mostly dressage and some jumping.

Reigna as a foal...

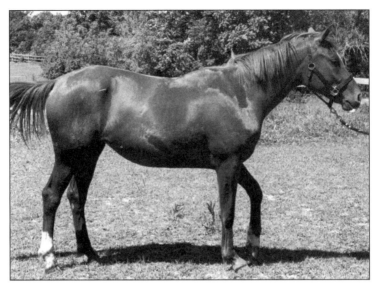

...and as a five-year-old.

My riding background includes eventing, hunt seat equitation, and dressage. Currently, both horses live at my home, and I ride them with the help of my trainer, as much as my time permits.

The pictures were shot on a beautiful February afternoon in Colorado. Thanks to the peculiarities in Colorado weather, you may notice the long, shaggy coats on the horses are in sharp contrast to my short sleeves.

Some cautions before we begin...

As you read this book, please realize that I am giving examples to be adapted to your situation. Learn the principles first, then apply the tools, and finally adapt them to your horse's personality and your own style. If you choose to use this book to provide yourself with knowledge and theory but feel more comfortable leaving the hands-on training to a professional, then by all means do so. Training horses can be dangerous and take extensive amounts of time. There is no shame in seeking professional training for you and your horse rather than trying on your own. In fact, if reading this book and other books on the subject convince you that starting horses is not your game, that's great. No one wants you to do anything that makes you uncomfortable. Furthermore, unless you are a professional horse trainer, you may not have the experience or the time to start a young horse or take your horse to the next level. Therefore, I encourage anyone who needs help to seek it out.

1

How Smart Are Horses?

Why is understanding the principles of learning important? Because we can use that knowledge both to predict a horse's reaction to various stimuli and to correct or prevent behavioral problems. Learning about behavior and cognition (the mental process by which knowledge is acquired) provides us with a greater understanding of the current trends in horse training and gives us greater satisfaction in dealing with our own horses every day. While the scientific study of learning is relatively new, the knowledge that we can train horses using positive reinforcement is very very old. The first principles of horse learning and behavior were described by Xenophon the Greek in the fourth century B.C. In his book *About Horsemanship*, Xenophon discussed how the environment and cues can produce learned behaviors and predictable behavior in horses. Xenophon promoted kind and non-coercive methods as the best way to teach horses.

Let us begin by thinking about the definition of *smart*. Words we can associate with smart include mentally alert, bright, knowledgeable, and shrewd. I think of smart as being a process. First, it is the ability to learn quickly, and second, it is the ability to remember what was just learned for a long period. We could extrapolate this further and say being smart includes taking that lesson, remembering it, and then applying it under different circumstances. Therefore, a smart horse is one that learns quickly and rapidly extrapolates that lesson so that it can perform that behavior in a variety of settings.

I think we can all agree that horses exhibit the ability to learn quickly and the ability to perform a behavior learned under one circumstance and repeat that same behavior in different environments. Therefore, we consider horses to be pretty smart. This is not a tremendous surprise considering that prey animals must be observant and have excellent memories to stay alive. In the wild, horses, as well as most other mammals, not only must avoid predators but remember where to find food and water. The horse that grazes too

Horses are alert to their environments.

close to a patch of tall grass and narrowly escapes a predator that leaps from the grass probably will not graze near that patch of tall grass any more. If the horse gets attacked near another patch of tall grass, he may start avoiding tall grass altogether. This demonstrates two important concepts in learning, acquisition and generalization. First, "If I graze by *that* patch of tall grass, I may get attacked," (acquisition of new knowledge) and second, "If I graze near *any* patch of tall grass, I might get attacked" (generalization of that knowledge to other situations). The horse has been **conditioned**, through punishment, not to graze carelessly near a particular patch of tall grass, and he has **generalized** that memory to other situations. The ability to learn and to generalize that lesson to apply to other situations has been essential to the survival of horses and many other species in the wild.

> ## At a Glance
>
> ### Principle
> • Horses are highly observant and aware of subtle movements in their environment.
>
> ### Tool
> • We can use subtle, consistent cues rather than large, coarse, or aggressive movements to teach our horses.

As a prey animal, horses are hardwired to learn survival behaviors very quickly. In addition, horses will react to new situations with the arsenal of behaviors and emotions that have suited them well in the past. As a result it may take a considerable amount of time to retrain or untrain a learned behavior.

Horses are highly social. Living in herds provides companionship and protection. Young horses learn not only social skills from their elders but survival skills as well. Anyone observing a group of horses knows how closely they observe each other. If one horse spooks, the rest jump along with it.

Horses are highly social.

Being minutely observant of each other's reactions helps protect horses in the wild by allowing the herd to escape danger. We exploit the horse's close attention to detail in our training. It allows us to influence their actions with such subtle cues as changing our arm position when lunging or round penning to indicate a switch in direction or shifting our body weight in the saddle to ask for gait changes. By understanding that your horse is always taking in what you are doing, how you are acting, and where you are moving, you will begin to understand why your horse reacts as he does. And if we can master how to read even a small amount of the horse's body language, the effectiveness of our training can increase exponentially.

As I've already mentioned, horses are incredibly observant of small details. However, the difficulties that arise in the horse-human communication highway typically arise because humans are not very observant of small details. This is our challenge. Humans are a verbal species, relying on sound and speech instead of movement and body language for communication. Humans often don't realize that horses pay far more attention to our movements and our posture than they do to the sounds we make. Take, for example, the story of Clever Hans.

Clever Hans

In the early 1900s Clever Hans, owned by Wilhelm Von Osten, became very famous in Germany for answering math problems. Von Osten would write a math problem on a black board and hold it up for Clever Hans to see. Clever Hans would then paw the ground the exact number of times as the answer (many of us have seen horses trained to do this today). Clever Hans gained such notoriety that a group of scientists was brought together to study him and determine just how smart he was. Oskar Pfungst led the charge. He compiled a series of tests for Clever Hans in an attempt to figure out whether the horse really knew math. He had Clever Hans answer math questions asked orally and questions written on a blackboard by his handler. These same tests were repeated using other handlers and by handlers Clever Hans could not see but could hear. In some instances Pfungst positioned the blackboard so the handler could not see the question but Clever Hans could. What they found was fascinating but in the end not very surprising. Clever Hans always answered the question correctly except in two situations: when he couldn't see the person asking the question and when the person asking the question didn't know the answer!

The inevitable conclusion was that the handler was somehow cueing the horse to start and stop pawing. Even when the handler was instructed not to move, the horse still pawed the correct answer. Interestingly, Clever Hans could paw out the correct answer not only for his owner but for just about any handler. Through careful observation Pfungst determined that when the handler lowered his eyebrows, the horse would start pawing and when the handler lifted his eyebrows, the horse would stop. Pfungst himself could make Clever Hans start and stop pawing at any time just by lowering and lifting his eyebrows. The humans handling Clever Hans had not realized that they were cueing him, the movement was so involuntary to them.

But why eyebrows? Well, just think about it. Whenever you concentrate on something, you naturally lower your gaze and eyebrows as you watch and think. This is the point at which Clever Hans would start to paw. As you approach the right answer, your gaze lifts in anticipation of the correct conclusion. When Clever Hans' handler recognized the correct number of paws, his manner would change and he would lift his gaze. At this point Clever Hans would stop pawing. Clever Hans was simply reading his handler's face and emotions and responding as his handler wished. It was all very simple to Clever Hans but required extensive study by humans to figure out what was happening. Who in this situation do you think was smartest?!

The story of Clever Hans offers several lessons. First, horses are highly observant, even of minute movements. Second, humans frequently misinterpret what they see. The scientific principle that we must remember is that we cannot accept a complicated explanation in a particular circumstance when a simpler explanation will do. It is far more likely that Clever Hans had learned to read his handler's body language (the cue) to start and stop pawing than it was that Clever Hans had learned to read numbers, learned what a plus or a minus sign meant, and learned how to do actual mathematical calculations such as addition, subtraction, and multiplication.

What we as humans often overlook is that even though we focus on oral communication, we are constantly expressing ourselves physically as well. The movement that was obvious to Clever Hans was subtle by our standards and required an astute scientist to pick up on and bring to our attention. We must remember that while we may not realize it, our bodies communicate a lot. We must also recognize that horses are more observant of the small nuances of movement that we express than we will ever fully comprehend.

Therefore, Clever Hans teaches us that horses are often cued by things we don't notice. For example, we may believe that we have trained our horses to come to the barn for breakfast when we enter the barn and open the feed bin. In reality, they may head for the barn when they first hear and see you open the front door to let your dogs out in the morning. I often hear horse owners tell of their experiences when they felt like their horse "read their mind." While we may certainly feel a spiritual connection to our horses, we must remember the lessons of Clever Hans and the fact that our horses may simply be paying more attention than we are. This coupled with their keen senses makes it more likely that your horse saw you come to the window and gaze fondly at him from the house. In response, he simply picked up his head to see what you were up to instead of him raising his head and looking in your direction because you were thinking of each other at the same time.

This awareness is also why we frequently think our horse is anticipating a cue while we are riding. We think we have trained our horse to canter with a specific leg cue, but if, for example, we always shorten our reins before asking for the canter, pretty soon the horse will canter as he feels the reins shorten.

2

How Horses Communicate

We know that horses communicate with one another, and we know that they communicate with us. The challenge is that sometimes we forget that when we are around our horses, no matter what we are doing, we are communicating with them.

As we have noted, horses are highly observant. This makes sense when you consider that a herd of horses can understand and interpret the alarm call of other species and thereby avoid danger. In addition, horses see humans as predators. We move and smell like predators. Therefore, horses consider us with some suspicion until trust is established. While all species use a combination of vocal and visual communication, it is important to remember that humans use mostly vocalization. In addition, because we are a predatory species, we move boldly and with confidence. This means that from a horse's point of view we are pretty loud and coarse. As a prey species, horses communicate largely through body language and observation. While they do communicate vocally, the majority of the time they are silent. Therefore, it is easy to understand why observation of movement is very important to horses as both a communication and survival tool.

The Senses

Sight

A horse's body and mind are highly geared for the observation of movement. The horse's eye is among the largest of any living mammal. The eye contains a tapetum (reflective surface) that increases the horse's ability to see in low light. In addition, the horse has more light-sensitive cells in the eye than humans have. This increased visual acuity comes at the expense of some color vision. While horses can observe color, they do not see as many hue variations as humans do. Color vision trials in horses support that they can distinguish among many colors and shades of gray. But they cannot distinguish between green and gray. In addition, hues of red and orange may also look the same.

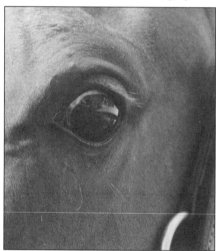

The horse has nearly 360-degree vision.

The placement of the eye is particularly interesting because it allows the horse to see virtually all around itself and have binocular vision in front. The shape of the horse's eye is such that objects farther away appear clearer than objects up close. Their peripheral vision is excellent, and horses can see movement at long range extremely well. Movement, in a horse's peripheral vision, may actually be accentuated. This is physiologic support that horses pay particular attention to even the smallest movements in their field of vision and may react quickly to something moving behind or to the side of them.

Hearing

Horses communicate through sound as well as through body language. A horse's ears are mobilized by 16 muscles, which help the horse locate the origins of sounds. Horses are also better than man at discriminating between noises of similar volume. Like dogs, horses can hear higher-pitched sounds than humans. However, the optimal sound frequencies for horses are similar to those for humans.

Smell

Horses are particularly keyed in to scents, which is not surprising considering they are prey animals. Prey species frequently use scent to discriminate between friend and foe since potential predators try to remain hidden until just before attacking. Horses use two organs for smell. First, they use nerve endings in the nose for the majority of scents. Second, they have a vomeronasal organ in the floor of the nasal cavity. This organ contains nerves that travel directly to the brain, specifically areas of the brain involved in behavior. When horses lift their lip in the flehmen response, they are directing air into the vomeronasal organ. Horses do this to get an especially good smell of something. This is a behavior that can be seen in all horses but is most frequently seen in stallions. Horses will do this most often when presented with a new scent. Stallions will also do this when sniffing feces left by competing stallions or when interacting with a mare in heat. You may be able to induce your horse to do it by wearing a new or unusual perfume to the barn.

Horses are very attentive to various scents in their environment. Scent helps them determine good versus bad foods, for example. Scents are important in sexual activity, allowing a stallion to determine when a mare is in heat, even from great distances. Chemical signals are also very important in individual identification, mare and foal bonding, geographical location, and in physical and sexual maturity. Scents can be potent markers of danger as well. You may have noticed how your horse treats sewer grates and ditches with great respect even from long distances. This is often more because of the smell than the physical appearance of the ditch or grate.

Types of Communication
Sound

Horses use neighs and whinnies to signal an individual's presence. We hear these sounds more when a new individual is introduced or a horse is being separated from a herd, prompting the horse and his former herdmates to call to each other.

Nickers are an invitation for you or another horse to come nearer. Nickers are most frequently heard from mares asking their foal to come closer. Squeals are a defensive greeting and often occur after nose-to-nose contact. Horses will also snort when alarmed and groan when they are tired. Horses that are very aroused and aggressive may roar or scream. Foals that are physically restrained may scream loudly when particularly panicked.

We know that horses will direct these sounds toward us as well as toward each other. My horses might whinny to me as I exit my house in the morning. I suspect that they are just reminding me not to forget to feed them. This announcement is followed by a more inviting nicker from my older mare, Margie, as I approach her with hay.

Horses are also willing to communicate with species besides humans. My dog, Buddy, has regular conversations with my horses every day. Buddy will invite Tieler to play by wagging his tail, barking, and running back and forth. Tieler will respond by lowering his head and pawing at Buddy. If they come to a consensus, they will take off and run up and down the fence line together. If they cannot, Tieler may turn and ignore Buddy or even offer a kick threat. If that doesn't work, Tieler may strike or kick at Buddy to get across that he is not interested in playing today. Reigna once had her nose under the gate to nibble on some hay scraps and Buddy approached her. As they touched noses, Buddy licked her. Reigna flattened her ears and squealed, letting him know that she did not appreciate it. In this case, Buddy's gesture was one of submission; however, Reigna interpreted it as being a little too personal.

It is fascinating to watch Buddy invite the horses to play and in turn to watch how the horses have learned to interpret his dog language. Buddy will run and drop down onto his elbows and bark. Tieler will drop his head and chase Buddy across the yard. While it looks like Tieler is truly aggressive toward Buddy, it is all play. Tieler rarely makes a very concerted effort to catch, step on, or kick Buddy even when Buddy would be an easy target. When neither of them feels like playing, they usually peacefully ignore one another. However, if Buddy crosses the line and invades Tieler's space, I have seen Tieler kick him just hard enough to get across his message.

Touch

Horses use touch to maintain their social structure. Grooming and mutual grooming are very relaxing to horses and serve to reinforce social bonds. Horses frequently nuzzle and rub each other's withers, necks, or manes. We have all seen horses extend their head and wiggle their lip as a pleasurable response to grooming.

Horses may nibble at another horse's face as an invitation

Horses frequently engage in mutual grooming.

to play. This may be followed by a romp across the field or play fighting, depending on the pair.

Touch can sometimes be aggressive. Horses will kick if another horse has overstepped its bounds within the social structure. Kicking is often preceded by a visual threat of aggression, known as a kick threat. A kick threat occurs when the horse picks up his hind leg and holds it there as if he is ready to kick. Not all kicks are preceded by a kick threat, and when intentional, a kick can be a swift and powerful form of communication. Horses can kick with either one or both hind legs. When a horse kicks with a forelimb, we typically refer to it as striking rather than kicking. Kick threats are typically reserved for herd mates and, by extension, humans or animals the horse is comfortable being around. This allows the intruder the opportunity to withdraw before being punished. When horses are faced with an aggressor or a predator, a warning does not precede a kick.

Body language

A horse will show excitement, fear, aggression, and appease-ment with body posture. Excited horses may roll or coil up their body in a very collected state, with the head tucked in and tail set high as they prance around. We typically see this behavior in stallions as they are led to a mare. Fearful horses will stand very erect with their head up to survey the land-scape and may snort or stamp a leg to warn the other horses in the herd. Aggressive horses will hold their head low to medium in height and flatten their ears. They may draw their lips back and show their teeth. If this warning is unheeded, a horse may charge. Horses may threaten each other by lifting a hind leg to demonstrate their willingness to back up their position with a kick. Similarly, if the threat is not respected a horse will usually follow through with an actual kick. (Horses will do the same thing to humans who fail to heed their warning signs or who startle them.) Submission by other horses is usually in the form of retreat, with the ears at half-mast and the head held low. Occasionally, foals will perform a chewing motion called snapping as an act of submission.

Showing signs of aggression.

It has been written that horses will lick and chew when they are con-templating a situation. Whether horses are actu-ally contemplating a situ-ation or not is really unknown. However, they do lick and chew as they become more relaxed. While working with your horse, you may find that licking and chewing precede a train-ing breakthrough. This is similar to a horse that is relaxed, accepting the bit, and has saliva foaming at his mouth while working under saddle.

Paying attention

Horses communicate with their human companions con-stantly. It is our responsibility to understand how our horse communicates with us in order to avoid misunderstandings. For example, if your horse regularly threatens to kick you when you pick up his hind feet you have several options in how you respond. If you ignore this behavior, he may escalate to out-right kicks, skipping the threat to communicate his dislike of your picking up his hind feet. If you retreat in response, he will likely continue to use the threat to prevent you from picking up his foot in the future. If, however, you recognize the warn-ing, establish dominance, and replace the horse's aggressive behavior with a desired behavior, you will stop the problem from progressing, and he will learn that he is to lift his foot qui-etly and obediently when you ask. When teaching the behav-ior initially, you may want to reinforce the desired behavior when he allows you to touch his hind leg without showing aggression toward you and then continue to shape the behav-ior until he allows you to pick up his foot. More discussion on behavior shaping occurs in the following chapters.

We must strive to pay particular attention to how we com-municate with our horse and how he communicates with us. We must understand how horses communicate with each other to be able to communicate clearly. We must strive to understand our horse's behavior as a prey animal, but, just as importantly, we must strive to understand how our behavior influences our horse's behavior. As in all relationships the key to success is open, honest, and clear communication.

3

Learning and Reinforcement

When we say that a horse has learned something, we are really saying that we have increased the likelihood that he will perform a particular action in response to a particular stimulus. However, a horse always has the choice of whether to perform a learned behavior because he still has free will. Therefore, in horse training we really have two goals: first, to condition (train) the horse to per-

At a Glance
Principle
• Horses readily learn but have the free will to choose whether to perform a requested action.
Tool
• Make your training more successful by using motivation.

form a particular action in response to a particular stimulus (cue), and second, to motivate the horse to perform that action each and every time that stimulus is presented.

Stages of learning

There are four generally accepted stages of learning that are applicable to both human and animal psychology. These stages are applied to the learning of a new skill:

1) **Acquisition**
2) **Fluency**
3) **Generalization**
4) **Maintenance**

You will become very good at recognizing these four stages as you teach yourself to carefully observe the process by which your horse learns a new skill. The first stage, **acquisition**, can occur quite rapidly, especially if you use the reinforcement techniques explained in this book. During the acquisition stage your horse will learn to associate the cue you have chosen with the behavior you are teaching him. At first he may only perform the behavior in one out of 10 tries, but soon he will perform it correctly in five out of 10 tries, and then almost always. He has then entered the stage called **fluency**, in which the cue is almost always followed by the desired behavior. During this stage we often refine the behavior, practicing it until the horse performs exactly as we want.

Once your horse is performing the behavior confidently and consistently, take the behavior out of the barn, arena, or round pen. You will now ask for the behavior in a different environment. You will likely experience some regression, that is your horse will not produce the desired behavior as reliably as before, but if you persevere, your horse will begin to perform the behavior when you request it under many different conditions. This stage is known as **generalization**. It is an important step in the learning process because a horse takes a skill he has acquired in one environment, such as the round pen, and understands he can perform that skill confidently in any environment, such as at a horse show or on the trail.

The speed at which a new skill moves from acquisition to

fluency to generalization varies, depending on many factors including the difficulty of the behavior you are attempting to teach. Simpler behaviors can be taught very quickly, perhaps in a single training session or two, whereas more complicated behaviors may take weeks to teach. In addition, the time it takes to complete a stage will vary with the number of times the cue is presented, the time between training sessions, the type of reward used, and the time between the performance of the behavior and the application of the reward.

Taking skills from the fluency stage to the generalization stage is a commonly overlooked step in training horses. I think this is largely due to laziness on our part. Once we have gone through all of the trouble to teach our horse a new skill, it is wearing to teach it all over again in a new environment such as an outdoor arena, on the trail, or at the show grounds. Then, too often, we get to the show and our horse reacts badly. We attribute our horse's poor behavior to his stupidity, and we become frustrated. However, if we understand that we must teach our horse in a variety of settings for him really to learn a skill, then we can avoid feeling frustrated and fix the problem before the show. In addition, you must move your horse's skills from fluency to generalization for him to progress to the next stage, maintenance.

Maintenance is the stage we seek for all the skills we teach our horses. At this stage our horse will reliably perform the skills he has been taught in a variety of settings. Sometimes animals appear to forget a particular behavior during the transition from generalization to maintenance. Some propose that this is due to the knowledge moving from your horse's short-term to long-term memory. What you will see is a regression in how he performs a skill for a few days. However, if you are patient and continue to practice, you will find that the behavior returns better than ever in a few days.

Moving a new skill from the generalization to the mainte-nance stage takes a relatively long time after the initial stages of learning. It could take months or longer, depending on how often the skill is practiced and how complicated the skill is.

Classical conditioning

The basis of studying animal behavior is knowledge of clas-sical conditioning, also known as **Pavlovian condition-ing**. Ivan Pavlov, a Russian researcher who studied salivation and digestion in dogs, would bring his dogs into a room and place each of them in a harness. His assistant would then bring in food and feed each of the dogs. The presence of the food would induce salivation, which Pavlov could collect and study. Pavlov soon realized that the mere sight of his assistant would cause the dogs to salivate, even in the absence of food. Intrigued by this behavior, he refined the experiment by sounding a buzzer just before every meal. Soon the buzzer alone stimulated the dogs to salivate. He called the food the **unconditioned** stimulus, because no training was necessary to induce the dogs to salivate at the sight of food. The buzzer became the **conditioned** stimulus or cue. Without training, the buzzer meant nothing to the dogs. But with repeated experience and the close timing between the buzzer's sounding and the presentation of food, the dogs soon associated the buzzer with food and would begin to salivate as soon as they heard the buzzer.

Do you think the dog would have salivated if the buzzer had sounded an hour before the food was presented? How about if the buzzer had sounded at variable times before the food was presented? The dog might eventually understand the connec-tion, but the response would not be consistent or strong. The ability of classical conditioning a sound as a cue to provoke an unconditioned response has been documented in almost all animals. From these studies, we have learned that the conditioned stimulus (buzzer) must occur before (not during or after) the presentation of the unconditioned stimulus (food) for an animal (or human) to associate the cue with the response. We have also learned that the cue must occur at a consistent interval and must immediately precede the presentation of the unconditioned stimulus to get the strongest response.

Now let us consider a situation in which the buzzer was so loud it frightened the dog. Do you think that the sounding of the buzzer would become associated with salivation? Probably not; however, the buzzer may become associated with fear. Conditioned cues may become associated with emotional responses as easily as they can become associated with movement or other reactions, such as salivation. When applying the above to training horses, we want to link our cues to physical actions within a positive emotional context. During a training session the horse's emotional state should be one of trust and comfort, not fear. Otherwise, we may

At a Glance

Principle

- For a stimulus to become conditioned (the buzzer for example), it must occur immediately before the unconditioned stimulus (presentation of food) for it to link to the ultimate action (salivation).
- Eventually, the conditioned stimulus alone will initiate the ultimate action (e.g., salivation) in the absence of the unconditioned stimulus (food).
- When applying classical conditioning to horse training, cues that evoke a fearful response should be avoided.

Tool

- Your conditioned stimulus (cue) will be something that is obvious, a sound or movement, but not scary.
- Remember the importance of timing and consistency.

inadvertently condition the horse to fear a stimulus instead of responding to it by performing a desired behavior. Compared to other species, such as dogs, horses are more easily conditioned to fear objects, sounds, or situations. As prey animals, this ability has kept horses alive in the wild. Therefore, it is our duty to be very careful in how we present and choose cues in order to decrease fear associations in horses. If we do this effectively, then horses will learn rapidly and learn to handle their fear.

Operant conditioning

So far, we have discussed the introduction of a cue (buzzer) to a stimulus-response scenario that already exists, that is seeing food initiates salivation. Now we need to discuss how we develop a stimulus response scenario from scratch. By this I mean we want to teach more complicated behaviors that will be performed by the horse in response to a cue such as leg pressure to initiate a canter.

The most common behaviors that we ask of our horses are an action or movement. The very first time you put a halter and lead on a foal and pull on the lead rope, the foal does not know that you want him to follow you. The pull is the stimulus or cue; the foal's following you is the response. We can develop this responsive behavior by using several tools. First, your horse must have a way of discerning desired behaviors from ones that we do not want. We will do this by **reinforcing** him. By reinforcing behaviors, our horse learns that if he responds to a cue, he will either be rewarded or punished.

When an animal learns that his or her initial action results in a reaction from you, it is called **operant conditioning**. That is, the final reaction operates on the initial action of the animal. We do this by reinforcement in the form of a reward or a punishment. The animal then discovers that its initial action will result in either a pleasant or unpleasant reaction. It is important to remember that rewards and punishments fall under the category of reinforcements and that reinforcements immediately follow the horse's action. Therefore, reinforcements influence the horse's preceding behavior by making it more or less likely to occur again.

Reinforcement

Typically, when we think of reinforcement we think of rewards. But the definition is broader. We use reinforcements

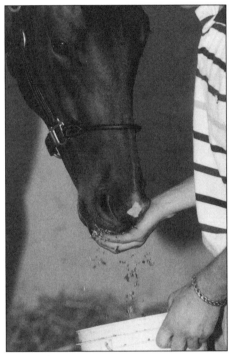

A treat can serve as a reinforcement.

to make desired behaviors more likely to happen and unwanted behaviors less likely to happen. We will use the term positive to mean we are *doing* something and the term negative to mean we *stop doing* something. Do not think of it as positive equals good and negative equals bad. It is more like math; when I use the term positive, I mean we are adding or putting something into the situation, and when I use the term negative, we are removing something from the situation. We'll use **rewards** to reinforce wanted behaviors and we'll discourage unwanted behaviors with **punishments**. Therefore, there are four terms we can use to describe the four different types of reinforcement: positive reward, negative reward, positive punisher, and negative punisher.

A **positive reward** is an action on our part that serves to make the preceding behavior more likely to recur, and it can be a treat, pat, rub, or other social behavior horses enjoy. We use the term positive because we are doing something to the horse that he likes. A **negative reward** also makes the preceding behavior more likely to recur. We use the term negative because as a reward we are removing a stimulus that the horse dislikes. For example, we may stop chasing him around the round pen or waving a rope at him. Other examples of negative rewards are when you stop pulling on a rein or squeezing with your leg.

Punishments are used to discourage unwanted behaviors. A **positive punisher** is the overt punishing act — we slap or hit the horse to discourage him from doing a behavior such as biting. In this case we are punishing him so we are applying something that he does not like. A **negative punisher** occurs when we take away something the horse likes — a buddy is removed from the pen, the horse's stall is shut so he cannot socialize with other horses, or his dinner is removed from the round pen. This is sometimes called a "time out."

What works best

In training any species, offering positive rewards is by far the best way to develop behaviors and maintain motivation. Negative rewards work well to teach behaviors but may not maintain as high a level of motivation as positive rewards. The use of positive punishment works least well. Why? Because there are more ways to do something wrong than right. Take our foal-leading example; if you pull on the lead rope because you want the foal to follow you, how do you reinforce the correct response?

Let me describe what might happen if you were attempting to teach a foal to lead using the four different methods we have introduced above. The following are four hypothetical teaching examples. However, in the end you will see that on a day-to-day basis we will use a combination of all four types of reinforcement to teach our horses. The behavior we are attempting to teach is the action of the foal stepping forward in response to you pulling on the lead rope.

1) **Positive reward**

You pull lightly on the rope; your foal resists and then takes a tiny step. You rub and pat the foal, maybe offer him a small tidbit of grain (if he's old enough), but you maintain the pull on the rope. You continue this process until the foal readily moves ahead when you pull on the rope.

2) **Negative reward**

You pull lightly on the rope; your foal resists and then takes a tiny step. You let go of the rope. You pause a second. You pull on the rope, the foal takes another step, and you release the tension on the rope. You continue this process until the foal readily moves ahead when you pull on the rope.

3) **Negative punishment**

You pull lightly on the rope; your foal resists. You turn your back on the foal and say nothing (you are removing social interaction with him as your punishment). The foal walks up and nudges you. You ignore him for a few seconds and then try again. You pull on the rope; your foal stands still. You turn your back on the foal and say nothing. The foal walks up and nudges you. You ignore him for a minute then try again. You pull on the rope; your foal takes a step forward and you continue pulling. The foal refuses to move forward;

you turn your back again…

4) **Positive punishment**

You pull lightly on the rope; your foal resists. You hit the foal for resisting. You pull on the rope; your foal tries to turn away. You hit the foal. You pull on the rope; your foal rears. You hit the foal. You pull on the rope; the foal leaps forward, shaking and sweating…

You can see from the above examples that rewards work better than punishments. I also hope you realize that we routinely use combinations of positive and negative rewards to train most behaviors. Most importantly, you must realize that using punishment will only create anxiety in your horse if you attempt to train simple behaviors with it. Punishment works best in countering aggressive behavior, which is only rarely encountered. Provided you treat your horse with respect and always expect respect from him, you shouldn't have major aggression problems. But if you do and you can't handle it yourself, better to seek out professional help in resolving the problem than risk injury. Remember your goal in the above example — we want the foal to be motivated to follow you when we pull on the rope. You will find when training horses that the combination of positive and negative rewards works best. So let's revisit our example again.

5) **Using positive and negative rewards together**

You pull on the rope and your foal resists. You are patient and keep light pressure on the rope. The foal steps sideways and you keep light pressure on the rope until he steps forward. You immediately release the pressure on the rope (negative reward) and praise the foal with a treat and a rub (positive reward).

In this example, we have established a behavior using multiple tools. By using two forms of reward, we will establish the behavior much more quickly than using only one.

Releasing pressure on the rope and providing a treat are both types of rewards or reinforcement that will encourage the foal to perform the movement again. Pulling on the rope lightly not only initiates movement, but also will eventually be interpreted by the foal as the cue to move forward (operant conditioning). Because of this, we want the foal to learn that light pressure but not hard pressure means move forward. From a safety point of view, light pressure is always safer than heavy pressure. Foals will readily flip over backward or leap into the air in fear or excitement when restrained with too much pressure.

At a Glance

Principle

- We use reinforcements (rewards and punishments) to encourage or discourage a particular behavior respectively.

Tool

- We use cues that initiate movement and then remove that cue as a form of negative reward. Positive rewards will encourage horses and foals to perform behaviors and will help maintain motivation.

Do you think the foal will learn to lead faster this way? If we punish the foal for every wrong direction he moves, we are going to be there a long time because he can go a lot of places besides forward. With all of that punishment, he may just stop trying. If we, or any animal, are repeatedly punished for trying to figure out the solution to a problem, it is a common response just to stop trying. This is called **learned helplessness**. Punishment is very effective in eliminating motivation. Positive punishment can also cause the foal to become overly frightened or aggressive. The unfortunate result of such a frightening experience might be that the foal associates the tug on the rope with being punished. Thereafter, pulling on the rope would trigger fear.

Our goal is to build motivation and have a foal that's happy to see us each morning and curious about what new things he will learn today. We want him to trust that the lessons we teach him will be fun and not frightening. From these training examples, we learn that motivation, confidence, and trust are closely linked.

Positive rewards	Negative rewards	Negative punishment	Positive punishment
Primary rewards:	Stop:	Withhold:	Inflict:
• treats • grain • carrot bits • apple bits • sugar • cereal • horse treats • rubbing • scratching • resting Secondary reinforcers: • clicker • verbal "good boy/girl" • kissing sound • any unique sound	• running after horse • nudging with whip • swinging rope • move yourself out of horse's personal space • making noises (clucking/kissing) • tapping, kicking, or squeezing with leg • pulling on rein • pulling on rope	• treats • affection • social interaction with you or other horses • remove feed	• pain by hitting, slapping with fist or object • fear by throwing, yelling, waving a scary object

Behavior Shaping

If we wanted to teach the foal purely with positive rewards, we would start by reinforcing a behavior with positive rewards and introduce the cue later, after the behavior has been established. This is opposite to the foal-leading example from above in which we started with a cue, pulling on the lead rope. We later removed that cue by ceasing our pull on the rope and used that as the negative reward. Pulling on the rope lightly is a soft cue and if done correctly should not frighten or cause injury to the foal. But if we could set up a situation in which the foal was following us anyway and then reinforce that behavior, we could teach the skill without ever having pulled on the rope in the first place.

For example, we could walk beside the foal as he follows his dam and reinforce this behavior.

At a Glance

Principle

• The process of behavior shaping occurs when you take a behavior and break it down into simple steps or components, and then reinforce the most basic steps and build on them until the final behavior is achieved. Each step is typically reinforced using positive or negative rewards.

Tool

• Begin training a new behavior by rewarding a small piece of it and then shape the behavior in succeeding steps into its final form.

Gradually, we will reward the foal for following us, then following us more and more closely. Once the behavior is established, we may add an oral cue such as "walk" or a subtle rope cue such as showing the foal the rope or holding the rope in a particular way to initiate the leading response. Reinforcing a behavior in steps and slowly altering it to exactly what you want is called **behavior shaping**. Behavior shaping using only positive rewards is commonly employed to train species that do not respond well to negative rewards.

For example, your cat may not come to you when you call and she certainly won't be enticed into coming to you if you chase her. But if you wait until she comes to you voluntarily and then reward her with a treat, you will find that she will come to you more often. You can then shape that behavior by adding the cue "here kitty-kitty" before rewarding her with a treat. You can further shape the behavior by only rewarding her when she comes at a trot instead of taking her time. In this situation there is nothing that you can stop doing that would reinforce your cat's behavior, so using a negative reward is not useful.

Fortunately, in training horses we can use both positive and negative rewards to shape behavior. This is largely because horses, as prey animals, are particularly responsive to running away from a stimulus. In contrast, a predatory animal is drawn to movement. If you started swinging a rope at your dog, he may either stand off a bit and observe you or take this as a game of catch the rope or tug of war. We will discuss behavior shaping in greater detail later in the chapter.

Searching and learned helplessness

We have also introduced another concept above in the foal-leading example. In several scenarios I stated that each time the foal felt the pull on the rope he did something different — he pulled back, reared, ran left, ran right, ran over the handler. All these reactions represent the foal's desire to figure out what the handler wanted. We call this varied behavior **searching**. As you train your horse, you will notice that searching behavior develops over time. Some horses enjoy searching; it becomes a game to figure out what the trainer is looking for. This is especially true once your horse learns that solving the puzzle will get him a big positive reward like a long scratch or a treat. If a horse is searching and gets positive punishment for each wrong "answer," he may soon stop searching all together. This is called

learned helplessness. You can imagine him thinking, "What's the point in trying to figure out what you want if all I get is punished for trying?!" But if, on the other hand, we can set up a situation in which your horse can realize that it is his job to search for the correct action in response to a new or novel cue, then learning could go very quickly. At this point you may be asking yourself; "So how do I respond to wrong answers?" You simply ignore them by not giving the horse any reinforcement (reward or punishment) and instead you allow and encourage him to continue to search for the correct answer. The other possibility is to employ a **conditioned punisher**. This is described in more detail below.

At a Glance

Principle

- When presented with a new or novel stimulus, horses will naturally try to search for the appropriate response. In contrast, if we punish our horse for incorrect behaviors when he is trying to figure out what we want, he may stop trying altogether, which is called learned helplessness.

Tool

- Give a searching horse time to figure out the appropriate response on his own by being patient.
- Try to ignore all incorrect responses and reinforce the correct one.
- Remember you can reinforce approximations of the correct response and then shape that into the final behavior.

Types of reinforcement

Let's talk about different kinds of reinforcers in more detail. Horses are inquisitive but generally very cautious animals. Because they are prey animals, some things that we might use to reward behaviors in both positive and negative ways might instead become linked to emotions such as fear. For example, one day you might wear a jingly bracelet. You could probably pet your dog all day long with your jingly bracelet on and she would not mind it a bit. But your horse might spook when you raise your arm to pet his head as he sees a bright, shiny, noisy, jingly thing coming at his face. At the least it could be very distracting. Your positive reward gesture (reaching up to pet him) has just become a form of positive punishment. Is this to say that your horse should not become adjusted to your wearing a jingly bracelet? Of course he should, but the point of petting him in this example is to reward him rather than to make him afraid of jingly bracelets. In this scenario we are trying to pet the horse as a positive reward for another behavior. We need to be cognizant of how we present ourselves to our horse and be sure that our intent is always embodied in our actions. We will cover teaching the horse not to be afraid of specific objects in the section on sensitization and habituation.

Primary and secondary rewards

Positive rewards may be **primary** positive rewards or **secondary** positive rewards. Primary rewards are the things you give the horse directly, such as a treat, rub, or resting time. A secondary reward is something you will have classically conditioned (remember Pavlov's dogs) to be a reward. By using classical conditioning you have taken something that means nothing to your horse, such as a sound, and conditioned your horse to associate that sound with a reward, such as food. We'll talk about secondary rewards at the end of this chapter in the section titled "The Power of the Secondary Reward."

As we have already discussed, rubbing, scratching, and rest are excellent primary rewards. However, I also use food rewards because they are practical and highly motivating. The best primary positive rewards are things your horse likes that are easy and fast to apply or offer. An example of an impractical reward would be turning your horse out onto a large pasture. Obviously, he would like such a reward but it is very impractical to turn him out after every correct response. The reward must also be something that your horse won't tire of or get satiated with. For example, giving your horse a pound of grain for each correct behavior would be impractical because after several pounds he would lose the craving and it would take him too long to eat it. In addition, it is unhealthy for him to have so much grain. And even though horses love grain, they often get grain without having to work for it. Therefore, grain may not be as special as a reward that your horse receives only when he is working for you.

> ## At a Glance
>
> ### *Principle*
> • Primary positive rewards should take many different forms: treats, rubbing, scratching, etc. They serve to bond you to your horse, maintain motivation, and reinforce desired behavior.
>
> ### *Tool*
> • Keep the treats small and handy for quick handouts, but never treat for free! Adapt your positive rewards to your horse's personality.

The positive reward you choose should be something that your horse loves but *never* gets when he is not working. Based on the above criteria, I use baby carrots as my primary rewards. I cut up the mini carrots into four to six pieces before my training sessions. One piece is a positive reward. My horses love them, and because I give them small pieces, they do not get satiated very quickly. For a special treat, I occasionally give sugar cubes. Other people use cereal, commercial horse treats, or grain. Remember, if you use grain, use only small amounts, and it works best if your horse does not get grain regularly.

There are some important things to remember about using treats. First and foremost, your horse should never get the treats for free. He must always work for them. This is a hard lesson for both of you, but it will prevent you from having to deal with a pushy, spoiled horse. No one likes a horse that bites and nibbles everyone who comes by. Treating sometimes gets a bad reputation because some people think that the horse will become a biter. Not true, if you stick to your guns and never give your treats for free! Never, ever, give in to a begging horse, or, worse, let your horse train you. For example, the horse nudges you and knowing that he must do something for his treat you respond by asking him to take a step back. You then treat him. Congratulations. Your horse has just trained you when to ask him for a simple task so he can get his treat.

Second, keep volume to a minimum. About a half-pound of anything is more than enough for any one training session. Have your treats ready, and remember you must treat within seconds of obtaining your desired behavior. I keep mine in a small, fabric nail pouch (the kind carpenters wear) wrapped around my waist. Once you are introduced to the secondary reward later in this book you will find that you won't use that many treats in your training sessions. In addition, you will eventually be rewarding only after the horse performs the behavior several times. This practice is called **intermittent reinforcement** and is very important in establishing behavior patterns. We will talk about it more at the end of this chapter.

You may think that a bigger treat is better than a small one, but generally the size of the treat does not matter. Surprisingly, it's *getting* the treat, not *eating* the treat, that is the real reward for your horse. For example, I have taught

Tieler to pick up an orange traffic cone with his mouth. When he picks it up, I take it from him and give him a small tidbit of carrot. I have seen him drop the carrot out of his mouth in his rush to pick up the cone again for another tidbit. Clearly, he is more motivated to get the tidbit than he is to eat it. Occasionally, if your horse performs a behavior extremely well, you may choose to give him a **jackpot**. A jackpot is a larger quantity of your usual treat or a special treat. This may be a small handful of carrots. By using a larger quantity of a reward, you are more likely to get your horse to perform that behavior the same way next time. Jackpots do not have to be food rewards. You may choose to give your horse an extra long rest or scratch as a jackpot, too. You should save jackpots for the rare occurrences when your horse makes an exceptional leap in learning a new skill. If you were to use them too often, they will have little meaning to your horse.

Your horse should learn that other positive rewards exist. Otherwise, one day you will be out of food treats and your horse will know it and decide to stop working. Scratching and rubbing your horse can be great rewards; just standing near you and having you swoosh flies away from him are great, too. Horses do not like to be patted and smacked (just try doing it to a foal sometime). Horses prefer rubbing and scratching, especially at the withers. Adult horses do learn to tolerate being patted, and some probably have learned that it is a positive reward, but why not start with something he already likes. A kind rub between the eyes, along the neck, at the withers, or on the chest is a great reward and provides social bonding. Though rubbing is a great reward, it is also something that you will do for your horse at other times. However, do not reward your horse while he is trying to bite or walk on top of you. He should be standing quietly and respectfully before you bestow your love and affection. While rubbing and treats are both good rewards, I find that treats are great for motivation and rubbing is great for bonding. Therefore, do not hold back on using both in your training program.

When choosing your arsenal of positive rewards, take your horse's personality into account. You want to choose rewards that encourage him but do not over-stimulate. I use my two dogs as an example. Darwin is an Australian shepherd who is highly motivated by food. When training him for agility, I tried using food rewards, but he became so distracted by them that he couldn't perform. He would drool and rush through his behaviors in his anxiety to get the treat. I found that play time, such as a short bout of tug of war, was a far better motivator. In contrast, Buddy, my Labrador, is barely motivated enough to stand up and get a treat from me. Playtime is definitely not motivation enough to get him to put in the extra energy necessary to get up from his dog bed and come over to me, so food rewards work better for him.

My horses have similar personalities. Tieler is often in my face and is typically the first to meet me at the pasture. Being male, he is inquisitive and prone to nuzzling and mouthing me anyway. With him I use treats very sparingly and focus on physical rewards such as rubs and scratching. I spend a lot of time reinforcing my personal space so that he respects it; using treats would only encourage a behavior that I'd like to discourage (entering my personal space without permission). Alternatively, Reigna is fat and lazy. She rarely canters off with the other horses in the pasture unless she is left far behind. Instead, she is happy to wait and see if they canter back so she doesn't have to catch up. For her, food in some situations is a much-needed motivator, and using combinations of food rewards and rest stops are her ideal positive rewards. You may find that your horse works best for a specific reward, such as a scratch on the shoulder rather than on the face.

Tools of the trade

Pictured here is a fabric carpenter's nail bag that I tie around my waist while I am working the horses. In it I can keep my secondary reinforcer, a small metal "clicker" device. I also carry my primary rewards. I prefer using mini carrots because I can cut them into smaller pieces and my horses

Clicker and carrots.

love them. Each small carrot divides into four to six rewards. I do not give my horses carrots at other times, so using them as a reward is extra special for them. Other foods you can use as primary rewards are cereal, sugar cubes, and small amounts of grain. Your primary reward should be small enough that your horse will not fill up on it and special enough that your horse stays motivated to work for it. Other non-food primary rewards include petting, scratching, and time to rest. These non-food treats are just as important as food primary rewards, and I don't always use my pouch when working with my horses.

Tieler accepting a primary reward

The photograph below shows Tieler working for a primary reward. I have asked Tieler to bend his head around to me as a stretching and obedience exercise. In the beginning the cue for teaching this behavior was lightly pulling on the halter rope. This pressure was released when he turned, which is a negative reward, and I pet or treat him as a positive reward. Eventually, standing in this position and touching his side with my hand or holding the rope out to the side will be the cue for him to bend around. This is an excellent exercise to

stretch your horse's neck. In addition, it is the first step in teaching your horse to perform a one-rein stop, to move his hind end over and face you, and for him to bend around your leg while under saddle.

Negative rewards

Negative rewards are used widely in many popular training

programs and are a powerful training tool. You can use them when round penning your horse to reward desired behavior. For example, you start swinging your rope and when your horse moves off at a trot, you stop swinging. This is commonly called "applying and removing pressure." Removing that pressure is the negative reward. In a round pen you can apply pressure by walking toward your horse, swinging a rope, yelling, or making loud noises — anything that makes him move. For a wild, unbroken horse, just being in the pen with him is applying pressure since he is not used to human presence. In this scenario the negative reward is the *removal* of that pressure. In the beginning you want to make the removal of that pressure as obvious as possible. For example, you stop swinging the rope while immediately backing up. Later, when your horse understands the negative reward, all you may need to do is lean backward and he will slow. Just about all of the aids we use while riding are examples of negative rewards. You pull on the rein and when your horse turns you reward him by removing the pressure. You squeeze with your leg and when he moves forward you stop squeezing.

Negative rewards are also a fast way of linking a cue to a movement. It is natural to use something that initiates movement in your horse as a cue. If you want the horse to go forward, wave a rope or a lunge whip from behind him. It is then very simple to keep this as your cue. But you can eventually choose to replace that cue with a whistle, an arm wave, or even a handstand simply by performing the new cue immediately before the old cue. Once your horse is performing the behavior consistently you can slowly eliminate the old cue.

The majority of behaviors we want to teach our horses involve movement: walking, trotting, cantering, turning, moving sideways, head up or down. Because horses are prey animals, they respond readily to pressure to create movement. We can therefore use this to our advantage when training. We create movement by applying pressure and reward that behavior by removing the pressure. Most traditional horse training programs use negative rewards almost exclusively for reinforcement of behavior. When riding, we use a negative reward when we pull on a rein and then release when the horse turns in response.

If you think carefully, you may remember a particular horse from your past that stopped poorly or would not go forward when leg pressure was applied. Why do you think the horse became that way? Either he was never taught what the cue meant or he became ambivalent to the cue because he was no longer rewarded for responding to it. Suppose a previous rider did not remove leg pressure when the horse responded by moving forward; instead the rider continued kicking or squeezing even when the horse moved forward. Eventually, the horse learned to ignore the rider and the cue. This is called **learned irrelevance**.

Learned irrelevance is a common problem in horses that are used for beginner riding lessons or in horses that are frequently lunged simply to get out some extra energy. When lunging a horse, we can easily forget to lower the whip or stop swinging the rope once the horse is moving. Instead, we continue to swing and swing, nagging the horse on. Soon, much to our annoyance, we find that our horse will not go unless we nag him. The horse has learned that the cue is "trot while she is swinging the rope" or worse, the horse simply ignores the handler because all he does is swing the rope no matter what the horse does. This is, of course, our own fault. We have failed on two levels. First, we have neglected to apply a positive reward and second, we have neglected to remove the applied pressure (negative reward). It is like telling your child over and over "clean your room, clean your room, clean your room, clean your room." And we all know how effective that is. I am sure you have seen such a horse: he starts around the circle and just keeps going without changing pace and without paying any real attention to the handler, doing whatever he wants on the end of the lunge line.

You can easily avoid the above situation by using either a primary or secondary positive reward system and by paying attention to your own actions. This will do two things. First, by applying the positive reinforcer, you will be adding a tool to your arsenal that will help your horse learn faster and stay motivated. Second, to apply your positive reinforcer, you will have to stop nagging your horse. In addition, by withdrawing the pressure of swinging the rope you are applying your negative reward. Remember, the benefit you will derive from using negative and positive rewards in concert is that your horse will learn much faster.

To review, let's discuss a more detailed example of using negative rewards. You want to teach your horse to face you in the round pen. First, in order for him to face you he has to move. Let us teach him that a particular place in the pen is his sanctuary. Place him in the pen and put yourself in the middle. When he is calm, start swinging your rope at him and he will move off. Keep swinging until he passes a particular point; as he passes that point, immediately stop swinging and back up. Placing an orange cone at that point will help you to be consistent. We do not care how fast he moves around the pen (do not pressure him until he jumps out of the pen, of course) or in what direction. Just make sure that whenever he passes that cone, you stop swinging and back up. If he does not pause at that spot, move him on again. In a few minutes he will slow at that spot, and soon he will discover that if he stands by that cone you will stop bugging him.

Once he moves to the cone and stands there, you can add your second condition. He must stand by the cone *and* look at you. When he is by the cone and staring at you, you continue to do nothing (this is a positive reward because you are letting him rest). When he looks away, move him off. If you consistently move him off whenever he is by the cone and not looking at you but leave him alone whenever he stands by the cone while looking at you, he will soon be standing there staring at you for longer and longer periods. This is an example of behavior shaping. You are shaping the movement from first having him slow and then stop at a particular point in the pen and then ultimately he must stop there, turn, and face you to receive his reward (he is allowed to stand and rest).

There are many variations to this procedure. Just think how using other positive rewards besides rest at each stage would help him learn what we want from him even faster. Remember, this is also an example of behavior shaping. We did not start with our goal. Instead, we started with something that got his attention and approximated our goal. We then shaped the behavior toward our final goal.

Photographic example of a negative reward

The photo on the opposite page shows the moment before I reward Reigna with a negative reward. I have moved toward Reigna while swinging my rope and she has responded by moving forward into the trot. As she is responding nicely, my next move is to stop swinging and moving toward her. This is the reward for her action or behavior. It is called negative reward because I am taking something away and stopping an action to let her know that she did what I asked her. This is a very common method of rewarding behavior in the round pen. An advantage is that you can apply it from a dis-

tance. In some situations you may only be able to apply either a positive or a negative reward. However, many behaviors lend themselves to being taught with positive and negative rewards in concert. This is advantageous because using two methods to reward your horse will help him understand what you want more clearly. This is because it will help your horse isolate which behavior you are seeking to develop.

Positive punishment

Positive punishment is not an effective way to teach a new behavior. This is because using positive punishment, such as hitting, slapping, or deliberately scaring a horse robs the horse of trust and confidence in humans. There are only a few situations in which positive punishment is called for, and they must be carefully chosen. The most appropriate situation is if a horse is violent toward a human. In this situation the level of violence directed toward the horse should be great enough to re-establish the human as the dominant animal in the pair. If punishment is excessive, your horse will respond in one of two ways. He may either become oblivious to punishment, the learned helplessness discussed earlier. Even if you escalate the severity of the punishment, the horse might never react. Or, he might become more aggressive toward humans. Aggressive horses are very dangerous and may be beyond rehabilitation.

The timing of a punishment is crucial. Ideally, punishment should take place the second the thought of aberrant behavior occurs to the horse. If the punishment occurs too late, you might inadvertently reinforce the unacceptable behavior. Suppose your horse is aggressive toward dogs and you want to eliminate this behavior. You decide that when your horse tries to attack the dog you will shout at him and, if he is within reach, hit him. But if you punish the horse after he has interacted with the dog, he may misinterpret the punishment as coming from the dog. In the future your horse will be motivated to attack the dog because he thinks the dog will attack him if he does not attack the dog first. In reality, because the timing of your punishment was late, your horse could conclude that the punishment resulted from the dog's approach, not the result of his attack of the dog. The difference is subtle but profound. If you continue to punish the horse in this way it is likely the horse's aggressive behavior toward the dog would escalate.

So how do you solve the problem? You could catch the horse before he ever takes a step toward the dog and correct him. This takes close observation of your horse's focus and impeccable timing. If you are uncomfortable with your ability to observe your horse and judge the appropriate time to correct him with a punishment, you may choose to block the unwanted behavior with a more desirable behavior. Instead of punishing him when he steps toward the dog, have him perform a different behavior, one that he knows very well, such as back up. If you have taught him to back up, have him back up immediately and positively reinforce it. You will hopefully extinguish the aggressive behavior by ignoring it and replacing it with a more acceptable behavior. This is called **counter conditioning**. In addition, seeing the dog will become a sign of opportunity for your horse. When the dog is nearby, your horse will associate her with the opportunity to perform a behavior and get a reward. In essence, the dog becomes a conditioned stimulus.

I am sure you have witnessed horses using positive punishment on each other. A mare will squeal and kick at a gelding or stallion making unwelcome advances, or a lead mare will chase another horse away from the feed bunk. Sometimes a threat alone will suffice. Horses will lift a leg or pin their ears at another horse and the submissive horse will retreat, usually with the dominant horse moving into the vacated space. This is called **displacement**. Using horse language to get your message across is far better than using a human interpretation of what constitutes punishment. For example, foals love to play and rear up, especially with Mom. However, I don't like it when a young foal rears up and mounts me. This is a perfect situation in which to use horse language as positive punishment. When the foal approaches me and starts (remember punishment after the fact is far less effective) to get light on his front end as if he wants to mount me, I will move toward him and push him away. I usually try to move to his side and push him away sideways by using my knee and thigh against his rib cage. I will do it pretty hard, but not so hard that he will fall down. If you do it too lightly the foal may interpret it as playing, and you will be rewarding the behavior. I do that once or twice and the little tyke usually goes back to trying it on Mom.

I use displacement on horses that have no respect for human space. A horse that walks over a human to get somewhere or that throws its head from side to side to strike a human in the head has no respect for that human. This is a very dangerous situation. A horse's head easily weighs between forty and fifty pounds, and if he swings it and you are in the way, he can give you a concussion. Horses that are higher in the pecking order of a herd will think nothing of bumping a subordinate out of the way. However, subordinates will rarely risk pushing a more dominant horse around for fear of punishment.

I have met many horses that walk all over their owners and would sooner run me over than stand still. I consider this inexcusable behavior, and it is a sign that the horse considers humans to be subordinates. There are many ways to establish a dominant position in your horse's mind. When you move a horse around a round pen, you are driving him as a dominant horse in the herd would. When you dictate his direction of movement, his speed, and the direction in which he turns, you are further establishing your dominance. When standing with a horse on the end of a lead line, I will often step toward his shoulder, forcing him to move over. That is, I have displaced him from his space. This is a subtle but powerful sign to him that I am the dominant person in this scenario. Since I have not hurt him physically in any way, I have also earned his trust. He can then see me as a leader, not as a predator that is to be respected only through fear.

Your ability to establish leadership through dominance and trust building will carry over into working with your horse in other situations. One subtle form of displacement occurs when you are standing in front of a horse and he is constantly moving his head from your left side to your right side without considering your space. Here he is dominating you. However, if you prevent him from swinging his head then you will be controlling his movement and establishing dominance. If I am standing by a horse's head and he tries to move his head to the other side of me without my permission, I will briskly put my hand up by his eye. If this does not work. I will hit the side of his head between his eye and his nose. Usually, the velocity of the horse's head hitting my fixed hand or fist is pressure enough to discourage the behavior without me having to throw a blow. Never hit a horse in his eye because you may damage it.

Physical (positive) punishment should never be employed lightly. When employed incorrectly, it can make an aggressive horse downright dangerous. The better alternative is to use dominant reinforcing activities (displacing your horse, controlling his movement) instead of physical punishment to get your point across. Appropriate behavior on his part can then be rewarded. In this way you will build trust, and your horse will see you as a leader. Physical punishment draws out the fight or flight response in your horse and can lead to aggressive, fearful responses. Even if you use horse language skills to get your point across, timing is still important. If you are trying to extinguish a worrisome behavior with punishments or rewards and it's not working or if the problem is getting worse, seek professional help.

Conditioned punisher

A conditioned punisher is similar to a conditioned reward in that it is a useful tool to modify behavior. I have already mentioned that using positive punishment to train new behaviors is less useful than the two forms of reward I discussed above, because there are more ways to do something wrong than right. Therefore, if we punish our horse with violence for every wrong choice he makes in the round pen or under saddle, he may become discouraged and stop searching for the correct answer. The exception to this rule is the conditioned punisher. The most common conditioned punisher used in natural horsemanship is the "two trips around the round pen" rule. Many trainers will "send" the horse around the round pen one or more times at a brisk trot or canter when the horse fails to perform a requested behavior. This punishment mimics how a dominant horse may drive a subordinate horse (displacement) to re-establish dominance over the subordinate. When a horse is first introduced to round pen training, he may not interpret running around the round pen as a specific punishment. However, by driving him around the pen we are establishing dominance over him, and soon he will look to us for leadership. He wants the human to tell him what he needs to do in order for the human to stop chasing him and let him rest. We then offer him a physical cue that conveys "would you like to stop, turn, and face me?" by backing up, and if he responds by turning toward us we reward him by letting him rest. If he fails to turn, we consider this a "wrong answer," and we send him on around the pen to create more motivation for him to turn and face us. He may search for the correct answer by turning to the outside or running faster, to which we respond by continuing to move him around the pen. Eventually, he will turn and face us, and we reward this with a rest, which is a positive reward. If sending him around the pen is used consistently for "wrong answer" when teaching certain behaviors, the horse will eventually learn to associate it with "no, try again." Similarly, if you request a behavior that your horse is already fluent in performing and he chooses not to perform it, you will use the trips around the pen to convey that you are still the dominant member of the herd and that he should reconsider. Therefore, a conditioned punisher is a nonviolent way to convey to your horse that the answer he gave was incorrect and causes him just enough discomfort that he seeks the right answer. By not using a punishment that evokes fear and anxiety, we allow him to use his brain to search for the correct answer.

Negative punishment

Negative punishment can be a great training tool and effectively take the place of positive punishment in some situations. If my horse is nibbling on me because he wants a treat out of my pouch, what is he really doing? He is attempting to train me! His cue is nuzzling; he hopes my response is to treat him. The choice is yours: you can let him train you or not. My choice is not, and in this situation I will either walk away and he gets no treat and no social interaction or I will displace him by driving him off. Then I may or may not ask him to work for his reward and happily treat or rub him.

Time-outs can be powerful in animals that are highly social. In her book *Don't Shoot the Dog!* Karen Pryor says that dolphin and whale trainers use time-outs as selective and effective punishment. This is an important point because you cannot slap a whale on the nose or chase it around the tank and have it feel punished! Marine mammal trainers use time-out only in certain situations, such as when a whale is getting too aggressive with a trainer. They pack up their fish and off they go. By removing the social interaction between whale and trainer, the whale is effectively dissuaded from that behavior in the future.

The technique can work well for horses, too, but it can also backfire. Horses are lazy and would rather do nothing than run around. If you use time-outs too often or for horses that are not motivated by human interaction, your horse may begin to interpret them as a reward. Your horse may be thinking, "If I try to bite her…she's going to leave and I get to stand here and relax!" So be careful. Use time-outs for only short periods (less than a minute), and follow them up with the opportunity for positive reinforcement. Carefully evaluate the situation to determine whether a time-out would be more effective than driving the horse away for a minute.

Photographic example of negative punishment

In negative punishment we use the term negative to mean we are taking something away from the horse. When using this type of punishment, we want to remove something that the horse likes. In this photograph I am withdrawing social interaction with Reigna because the behavior she performed immediately before this moment was unacceptable. As you can see from the look on her face, this is not a very effective punishment. First, she looks quite relaxed and happy to be left alone. Under some circumstances she may interpret being left alone as a reward. I find negative punishment

works best for begging behavior. If a horse is nudging and entering my personal space trying to get food from me, I will withdraw my interaction until the horse minds its manners. However, if the horse is being aggressive, you should respond with a similar amount of force so as to maintain your status in the herd. One choice is to displace the horse by moving him out of your personal space.

The power of the secondary reward

Here is a problem: you want your horse to stop by the cone that you placed near the outside of the round pen and look at you. You are using negative rewards (you stop swinging the rope when he goes near the cone), but you want to add a positive reward to your tool kit to make him learn the behavior even faster and with better motivation. But when he is standing at the outside of the round pen, it takes several seconds for you to walk over and give him a treat. In the meantime he may take off. What we need is a positive reward that can be applied from a distance and at the exact moment the horse is doing what we want.

We do this by using a secondary positive reward. A secondary reward is something that usually means nothing to the horse, such as a sound, that has been **conditioned** to be a reward. Have you ever seen a dolphin jump out of the water and have the trainer reply with a whistle or clicking sound? How about a dog trainer using a metal "clicker" to reward the dog? These are examples of secondary rewards. You can use a mechanical noise such as a metal clicker, a whistle, or a very specific word spoken in a particular tone of voice. My horses are conditioned to both a clicker and the word "good."

You condition your horse to the secondary reinforcer (a clicker, word, or action) by classical conditioning. It is a very simple procedure. You click or say the word and immediately treat, wait a bit, and then click and treat again. You repeat this over and over until you have done it 20 to 30 times or more. You should wait varying periods of time between click and treat sets. The treat must always come immediately after the click, but the time between clicks can vary. This is very important because we do not want the horse to associate any particular behavior with the click and treat. For example, you do not want him to learn that standing in front of you and staring at your hand is how to get you to click and treat him. He must be doing different things when you click and treat so that the click will become synonymous with the treat. Horses clue in to this very quickly. It only took two or three sessions before my horses understood. You may also condition your horse to associate a word as a secondary reward. The process is the same except you would say the word and then treat and do this over and over until your horse recognizes the word and comes to you for the reward.

Once your horse understands the secondary reward cue (click or spoken word), you will notice that he may stop doing whatever he is doing and come to you when you apply the secondary reward. I will accept this in the beginning, but soon I will insist that the horse continue to perform the activity until I invite him to get his reward. Your horse will make this transition naturally when you move him from a continuous reinforcement schedule to an intermittent one. That is you change from treating him every time he hears the secondary reward to only occasionally. We will discuss reinforcement schedules below.

Reinforcement schedules and jackpots

Have you ever gone to a casino and played a slot machine? Why do people sit hour after hour playing a single slot machine? The answer is **intermittent reinforce-**

ment. If you were positively rewarded every time you did something, we would call that a **continuous reinforcement schedule.** For example, if you put money into a slot machine and won every time, not only would you be very happy, you also would be on the receiving end of a continuous reinforcement schedule. If suddenly you stopped winning each time, how long would it take for you to give up putting quarters into the machine? Maybe it would take 25 to 50 times. This loss of behavior is called

> ## At a Glance
>
> ### *Principle*
> • Intermittent rewards stimulate continued performance of behaviors even in the absence of a reward for each individual performance of the behavior.
>
> ### *Tool*
> • Use continuous rewards to teach a new behavior and then move your horse to an intermittent schedule once the behavior is established.

extinction. In the beginning you quickly figure out that putting quarters into the machine is good. However, when the reinforcement is removed, it takes only a small number of unrewarded tries for the behavior to **extinguish**.

Now, if you sat down at a machine and started putting quarters in and you won every time for 50 times in a row you would probably be pretty glued to that machine. What if the machine then put you on an intermittent reinforcement schedule? At first you would win after every five attempts *on average*. That is you might win after two, three, four, six, seven, or eight tries. There would be no pattern other than you would win on average every five pulls. Then unbeknownst to you it might become on average every 10, 20, or 30 pulls before you would win. Because there was no pattern you would continue to play never knowing which pull would yield the big prize. Do you see how this can be applied as a powerful training technique? Then, to add fuel to the fire, once in a while you would pull the handle and get a really big prize. A jackpot! You are now really hooked on your machine, never knowing when you will win a small prize, or even better, a **jackpot**. What if we stopped reinforcing you completely? How long do you think it would take you to stop playing? Remember, under the continuous reinforcement schedule it took only a few more pulls for your behavior to extinguish. But this time, because of the intermittent schedule it may take hundreds of pulls before you give up and leave the machine. Such is the power of gambling.

Applying these principles to teaching your horse a new behavior will establish it more quickly. In the beginning you will use a continuous reward schedule until your horse understands the basic idea of the behavior. Then you will move him to an intermittent schedule of reinforcement. By doing this, you are really "cementing" the behavior into his brain. That is you are making the behavior more resistant to extinction. However, you do not want to move on to an intermittent schedule until you have used a continuous schedule for at least 50 to 100 trials and/or your horse really understands the behavior you want.

Unfortunately, intermittent schedules can make it very difficult to extinguish an unwanted behavior for the same reason intermittent schedules are desirable for wanted behaviors. Take for example, a child that does not want to go to bed at a certain time. When it is time to go to bed, the child cries and carries on. Sometimes the parents do not have the energy to force the child to go to bed and so give in and let the child stay up for an extra half hour. Other nights the parents insist and the child must go to bed. This is an intermittent schedule; some nights the child's poor behavior is rewarded by being allowed to stay awake, while on other nights the child must go to sleep. After months of this the parents decide that from now on the child will always go to bed at the set hour no matter what the child's behavior. The parents will probably find that the child's bad behavior escalates for several days before the child learns that no matter what happens he/she must go to bed at the set time. This increase in intensity and/or frequency of behavior starting

> ## At a Glance
>
> ### Principle
> - If you are trying to extinguish a behavior that was previously rewarded, you will experience a surge of the behavior before it begins to extinguish.
>
> ### Tool
> - Stick to your guns. Know it will get better after the surge is over will help you maintain your conviction.

after rewards are withdrawn is typical before a behavior starts to extinguish.

If you let your horse teach you that when he nuzzles you he gets a treat and you decide to extinguish that behavior by not treating him no matter what he does, do not be surprised if he starts to nuzzle you harder and harder and perhaps even try to bite you (behavior intensification) before he stops nuzzling you. In addition, after a period of time without nuzzling he may all of a sudden start nuzzling and trying to bite you again before the behavior is finally extinguished. This is called **spontaneous recovery** and is discussed more fully in the next chapter under flooding.

Photographic example of a jackpot

In the photo on page 68, Reigna receives a jackpot for a particularly good response to a cue. Jackpots may be a very special treat like a sugar cube or a larger number of your usual

treats. Here she gets four whole baby carrots as opposed to her typical one-quarter of a baby carrot. Jackpots are particularly good at rewarding a training breakthrough or boosting your horse's motivation. Reigna is very lazy, so when she gives me an energetic response I try to reward that behavior with a jackpot. Jackpots should be used sparingly, just a few per training session and only if truly warranted. I may end training sessions with a jackpot after the horse performs something particularly well. The old adage, finish with something easy, something the horse knows well, still holds true.

Tieler coming to me for his primary reward

In the photo on the opposite page, Tieler comes to me for his primary reward after hearing his secondary reward. When you introduce a secondary reward, such as the phrase "Good boy!" or a sound like the one from a "clicker" device, you will know the horse has made the association when he stops whatever he is doing and comes to you for the treat. In a round pen situation the reward is on several levels. First the

horse hears the secondary reward, then he comes in for a treat, and, while there, gets to rest, all of which reward his good behavior. Eventually, you will put your horse on an intermittent schedule of reinforcement. You will ask him to perform a behavior several times, for each correct behavior he will hear the secondary reward, but intermittently the primary reward will follow the secondary one. In this way, he will not interrupt the flow of your work by entering the middle of the pen for every reward. Eventually, you will also use the secondary reward intermittently.

Behavior shaping

When starting to teach your horse a new behavior, you may not be able to start with the complete behavior, especially if the behavior you are trying to teach is complex. Let us revisit the traffic cone example under the context of behavior shaping. In order to teach Tieler to pick up the orange traffic cone with his mouth, I might have found myself standing for many hours with him and the cone watching him nudge it and kick it before he ever thought of picking it up. It was also highly possible that he would find the cone uninteresting, in which case I would have spent many hours watching him ignore the cone without any opportunity to reinforce the desired behavior.

We can overcome such a dilemma by teaching the end behavior in steps. This is called **behavior shaping**. Behavior shaping is a very fast way to teach new skills and an excellent way to refine existing skills. I also find behavior shaping to be a fun way to teach your horse something new. Let us return to my idea of teaching Tieler to pick up the orange cone. The first thing I did was put the cone on the ground. When he sniffed it, I clicked (using my established secondary reward) and he got a treat. By using my secondary reward, I could reinforce the exact behavior I wanted. In this case, it was having his nose near the cone. Once he was doing this consistently, I set my goal higher. Now, I only clicked and treated when he sniffed the top of the cone. When I stopped rewarding him for sniffing the bottom of the cone, Tieler began searching and sniffing other parts of the cone. When he sniffed the top of the cone, I rewarded him. I continued to reward sniffing the top of the cone. Then I stopped rewarding sniffing. This induced him to search and he tried nudging the top of the cone with his lips and I rewarded this behavior. Eventually I moved on to rewarding him when he mouthed the cone, then bit the top of the cone, and finally lifted the cone up off of the ground. At this point I put Tieler on an intermittent reinforcement schedule by clicking and treating, on average, every five lifts of the cone. Behavior shaping can be a fast, fun way to teach your horse some behaviors. For example, I taught Tieler to lift the traffic cone in two training sessions.

I could further shape the behavior by rewarding him for standing and holding onto the cone for longer periods, handing the cone to me, or throwing the cone. The choice is mine. Behavior shaping is a lot of fun, but you should decide what your final behavior goal will be and how you will get there. A frequent problem for trainers is that they do not break a behavior down into simple enough steps. For example, if your goal is to teach your horse to load onto a trailer, you might decide that your first step is to reward him for stepping onto the trailer with one foot. However, your first step should be to teach him to move forward in response to a cue.

Your horse may also attempt to guide you in the final outcome of your behavior shaping due to his or her personality. This is fine if your goal is to teach a silly trick. For example, Tieler loves to pick up the cone whereas Reigna prefers to kick it around. Therefore, I have shaped Tieler to pick up the cone and Reigna to knock it down and put it back up again. However, if you are teaching a more complex behavior, you may be more discriminating. For example, if you are interested in dressage you will want to shape a canter transition to be very precise while your horse's body remains straight as opposed to accepting any transition no matter how your horse gives it to you.

Once the behavior is established, you can also refine it by adding a cue. For example, Tieler would only get a reward if he lifted the cone after I said, "take" or "cone." I can also refine this behavior by rewarding or jackpotting the fastest lifts, the lifts where he shakes the cone, or the lifts he performs farther away from me. You may shape a behavior in any way you wish, provided you are consistent in your final desire. Try not to start to teach your horse to pick up a cone and fling it across the ring and then switch to having him hand it to you. It may be confusing for your horse and painful for you in the event he throws it at you!

Behavior shaping is especially important for teaching behaviors under saddle. If you are teaching a canter departure, you may start by reinforcing any and all departures. Over time you may start rewarding only the best departures and then the fastest or most balanced. For example, Reigna had a nasty habit of dropping her head and pinning her ears when I asked for a canter departure. I used behavior shaping and rewarded only the better departures. Over time she would occasionally depart without the dropped head and pinned ears. Those departures got a jackpot. In this instance my jackpot consisted of immediately using my verbal secondary reinforcer, "good," then letting her stop cantering (negative reward) and giving her several carrots (primary

I shaped Reigna's behavior in steps so that she eventually could knock over the cone.

I shaped Tieler's behavior first to mouth the cone...

reward). By rewarding good behaviors and ignoring the less desirable versions, I extinguished the dropped head and pinned ears in favor of a good canter departure. Today, the intermittent reinforcer of the oral "good" is all I need to do to maintain the behavior.

Another example of behavior shaping is teaching complicated maneuvers, such as a sliding stop or a turn on the haunches. We start by rewarding an approximation of our ultimate goal. For example, we reinforce a fast halt or the horse moving his front end away from leg pressure. We can continue to shape each behavior until we get what we want. In these situations we are using shaping for behaviors that take muscular strength to perform. It is unfair to train a dressage horse to do a *piaffe* (trot in place) in one day. The pain and muscle stiffness that would result would be punishment enough to make him never want to try it again. Instead, we develop the behavior over time by gradually increasing his collection at the trot. With each lesson, he carries more weight, developing

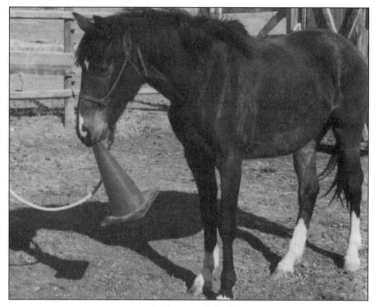

...and then pick it up.

his musculature. Plus, he has the time to decipher what it is you want and exactly how you want it. The result is a light, even *piaffe* without resistance or muscle or hock soreness. Complex behaviors or movements such as the *piaffe* or the sliding stop take months, if not years, to perfect and when given time to develop, the results are spectacular.

In the preceding paragraphs I have illustrated how behavior shaping can work quickly, as with the cone trick, and in the development of complex movements. Behavior shaping is therefore a very powerful teaching tool.

4

Behavior Shaping
Sensitization, Habituation, and Flooding

When presented with a new stimulus such as a swinging rope, plastic bag, or ringing bell, a horse may respond in several ways, depending upon his experiences. Typically, a stimulus that is loud or unusual evokes alarm. This triggers a massive release of adrenaline that results in many physiologic reactions such as dilation of the pupils, increased heart and breathing rates, and increased blood flow to the major muscle groups, all in preparation to flee from whatever the horse perceives as life-threatening. Horses in the "flight or fight response" are reacting with fear and thinking only about self-preservation. When horses confront new or unusual objects or situations, they will normally react with some fear. However, if the object is presented in such a way that the horse's fear is not substantiated, then he will learn not to fear that object and will gain more trust in the human who presents that object. If an object is presented too rapidly or in such a way that the horse becomes injured, then the horse may become excessively fearful of that object. This is called **sensitization**; in other words, we say that the horse has become sensitized to that object. Because horses are prey animals, they are particularly good at becoming sensitized to objects. This is a behavior that can keep them alive in the wild. When a horse is used to an object or situation without being afraid of it, he is **habituated** to it.

Therefore, avoiding the fight or flight response is in our best interest when training a horse. This presents a dilemma because we want our horse to learn how to handle his fear. We do this in two ways. First, we expose the horse to potentially frightening objects in a gradual manner. This is called **gradual habituation**. Second, we encourage the horse to turn and face objects that he is fearful of without running away. Our goal is to **desensitize** the horse to that stimulus and then **generalize** that experience so that when presented with it again, he will either not react or turn and face it. This is a tall order in a prey animal but can be accomplished using the tools we have discussed.

Many trainers refer to acclimating a horse to potentially scary stimuli as "sacking out." Rustling plastic bags, flapping flags, swinging ropes, clanking chains, and running tractors are just a few of the things to which we would like to accustom our horses. Desensitization may be accomplished in three different ways: gradual habituation, flooding, or counter conditioning. Gradual habituation is a slower process than flooding, which is accomplished very quickly. Habituation is the introduction of a stimulus that has the *potential* to terrify our horse. If this process is done gradually and in steps, the horse will habituate to the sound, object, or situation.

Sensitization and desensitization

Attempting to habituate a horse to a new stimulus can provide plenty of opportunities for things to go wrong, especially if accidents happen or if the procedure moves forward too quickly. This happens to many horses when their owners or handlers attempt to "teach them to tie." When a horse is tied and first pulls back, he will feel trapped and may panic. His panic can cause him to struggle against the restraint and fling objects about as his handlers shout at him. Eventually the halter, rope, and post break, and he is set free. He has also experienced great fear because of the noise and excitement associated with his panic and the feeling that he could not get away. The next time the horse is tied he likely will fight the tie sooner and more aggressively than he did the first time. Once sensitized to a stimulus or situation, habituating the horse to that stimulus will become much more difficult than if the horse had never become sensitized to it in the first place. For example, if you taught your horse to give to pressure exerted on his halter, and that behavior was generalized, then your horse would give as soon as he felt the tie rope pull on his halter and he should tie without a problem. Some people believe that you can successfully teach this skill in the first hours and days of life so that unfortunate scenarios such as described above will not happen.

> ## At a Glance
>
> ### *Principle*
> - You can habituate your horse to all types of threatening objects and situations in a controlled setting so that when he encounters them again he will not respond with fear.
>
> ### *Tool*
> - To avoid inadvertently sensitizing your horse to an object or situation, it is imperative that you do not go too fast. Several short training sessions over a few days are better than trying to accomplish the habituation in one long session.
> - Reinforcing the good behavior of your horse with positive rewards will help bolster his confidence.

If you attempt to sensitize a horse to a plastic bag, you might just walk right up to the horse and shake the bag vigorously in his face. The horse would likely spook and run away. If you did this just a few times, you would probably find that just walking into the round pen with a plastic bag would send your horse flying to the other side with a loud snort. Congratulations — you have just sensitized your horse to plastic bags. Note that his reaction now is much stronger and filled with more emotion than the very first time you presented the bag to him. Obviously, I do not recommend that you do this! Therefore, let us take our plastic bag as an example and look at three methods of desensitization.

Habituation

Say that you would like to habituate your horse to a large plastic bag. Place your horse in the round pen at liberty and stand several feet from him so that he has room to move away from you if he chooses. Crinkle the bag and carefully observe your horse's reaction. If he panics, that was too much pressure and you will need to back off, perhaps crinkle less vigorously, or put more space between you and the horse. If he just stares at you, you can apply your secondary reward. You have already applied your negative reward by stopping the crinkling when your horse just stood and looked at you. If your horse moves off or does not turn to face you while you are making the noise, consider sending him around the pen once as a conditioned punishment. However, do not move him around the pen by chasing him with the bag. After a trip around have him face you and crinkle the bag again. You will want to repeat this procedure until he turns to face the bag and not run away. When he has accomplished this, move toward him and crinkle the bag again. Continue this process until you can rub the bag all over his body while he is standing still. Depending on the temperament of the horse, this may take five minutes to several sessions or longer. This same procedure is followed for other objects, including equipment you plan to use on the horse such as saddle pads, halters, etc. Once your horse accepts these items within the round pen, the procedure should be repeated in other settings to help the horse generalize the behavior of how to handle fear. Let your horse's reactions guide how quickly you progress; you never want to invoke the flight or fight response. It is better to go too slow than too fast.

I do not recommend that you try to habituate your horse to something scary while he is tied, is on a lead, or is in a small space. In order to feel comfortable, the horse must feel that he can escape. If he feels that he cannot move away, the stimulus in the context of a confined space may trigger the fight or flight response. Once you have introduced several scary objects this way and successfully habituated your horse, you will find that subsequent new articles will habituate much more quickly. Your horse is learning how to handle his fear and have faith and trust in you. Now is the time

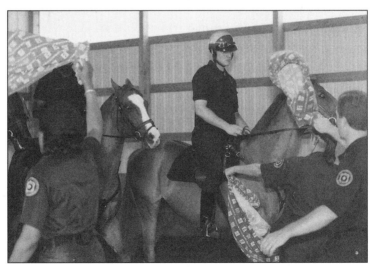

Habituating police horses to plastic bags.

to introduce objects outside the sanctuary of your round pen or arena. Your horse must learn to **generalize** his experiences to other environments. In these scenarios he will likely be under saddle or on a long line, but since he knows the game and provided you go slowly, things should be fine.

Some horse trainers perform impressive acts of habituation in front of large audiences in a few minutes to a few hours. They will be the first to tell you that while it is impressive, horses need to see these objects over and over again for their behavior to generalize. Generalization is what allows your horse to overcome his fear of all plastic bags, not just the one in your hand in the round pen.

Flooding

Flooding is a quicker form of habituation, but can go very wrong and have the opposite effect of sensitizing a horse very quickly. However, this method can be very useful if you pick your cases carefully. **Flooding** exposes the horse to the offending stimulus whether he likes it or not. You allow him to get scared and keep exposing him to the stimulus until he calms down and accepts it. This may take quite a while and the horse must be in an environment where he will not injure himself or you. A simple example of flooding is teaching a horse to accept being tied by tying the horse via his halter to a fixed post and letting him fight until he gives up, stops fighting, and just stands there. It may take a few flooding experiences before he accepts being tied and stops pulling back each time he is tied. Obviously, there are potential problems with this example. As a veterinarian, I have seen horses fight so hard that they tear muscles in their hind end or flip over backward and fracture their skull or break a leg. More often the horse panics and breaks the fence, pieces of it flying everywhere. The broken boards and noise scare the horse even more. Now you have a horse that is sensitized to tying, which makes the job of teaching him the behavior all the more difficult. Therefore, I am not a fan of this method of teaching a horse to tie.

I have also heard of taking horses into deep sand, water, or snow, or placing them in a stock to limit their ability to hurt themselves and then flooding them. You can use this technique for everything from head shyness to saddling and backing. However, there are several things to remember about flooding. First, it is not a do once and everything is fixed method. You may need to do it two or more times for the experience to become generalized and in some cases the

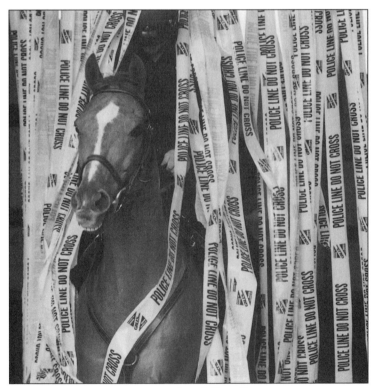

An example of flooding.

behavior may still return, a phenomenon called **spontaneous recovery**. Second, if you do not follow through, that is if you stop while your horse is in the middle of the fight or flight phase, you inadvertently will be rewarding his behavior, resulting in a sensitized horse. Third, as your horse panics, he may injure himself or the people around him.

In my opinion, gradual habituation is safer for you and your horse and has a longer lasting effect on the horse. Flooding is tempting because it seems to be the great quick fix, but in reality you may have to do it more than once, adding

At a Glance

Principle
• Gradual habituation and flooding are methods to teach your horse not to be afraid of various items and situations.
• A sensitized horse is always more difficult to habituate than one not previously sensitized to a particular stimulus.

Tool
• Gradual habituation is a safer and longer-lasting method, in virtually all situations, to teach your horse to tolerate various stimuli.

greater risk of injury to the horse or handler. In addition, horses that have been flooded may occasionally revert and regain their fear response (spontaneous recovery). With gradual habituation your horse may revert a step or two in the process but usually not to ground zero. Remember that gradual habituation and flooding work far less effectively in a horse that has been previously sensitized to a stimulus. It is much easier to start with a clean slate.

Habituation, whether done gradually or through flooding, can be used to get horses acclimated to many different environments and objects. The more objects or situations your horse is exposed to the better able to cope with new situations he will be. An extreme example of this would be police horses and in the past, cavalry horses. These horses are trained to withstand extreme numbers of people, noises, and gunfire.

Counter conditioning

Counter conditioning is training your horse to perform a well-learned behavior in lieu of an undesirable one. With respect to desensitization, you will use counter conditioning to help your horse regain his composure and overcome his fear. For example, some horse trainers will teach a horse to stop on a particular cue, such as quickly pulling back on one rein (the one-rein stop). Once your horse has learned this cue and developed the behavior to the maintenance stage, you can use it in situations in which your horse becomes frightened. By applying the cue, the horse will automatically perform the behavior before he has a chance to overreact to the fearful stimulus. Using a cue and behavior that your horse does not know very well will not work. The fear stimulus will override the horse's desire to respond to the cue. Behavior responses that have achieved the maintenance level are almost automatic, and the horse will often respond to the cue no matter what the situation, giving the horse and rider a few seconds to regain their composure.

Imprinting

Imprinting is a form of flooding whereby a newborn foal is held by a human and then desensitized to various stimuli. Most commonly the foal becomes accustomed to being touched all over its body. During imprinting the foal is held and not allowed to move away. The foal is then rhythmically rubbed over its head, mouth, and limbs. The bottoms of the feet are tapped to simulate a farrier's use of a hammer and for cleaning. As imprinting is a form of flooding, we may want to take what we know from our experiences in flooding adults and apply it to foals. In adults a one-time exposure using flooding may not necessarily be enough to accomplish desensitization, and repeated exposures to an object might be necessary to achieve desensitization *and* generalization. However, proponents of foal imprinting relate that repeated exposures are often not necessary in foals. This may be because we are taking advantage of a critical learning period.

In some species, imprinting is defined as a very specific phenomenon. For example, in many species of birds, the hatchling "imprints" on the first moving object it sees after birth. The hatchling considers this object its "mother." The "mother" is usually the mother bird but can also be a human, another animal, or even a puppet. The imprinting

Imprinting a foal.

occurs during a specific period in which the hatchling is said to be receptive. Outside of this sensitive window of time the hatchling will not imprint. From this example we can conclude that foals do not truly imprint in that they do not imprint on inanimate objects and consider them to be their mother. However, from a scientific point of view it remains unknown whether foals have a period during the first three hours after birth when they are particularly susceptible to learning. This is called a **critical period** or **sensitive phase** by some researchers. Newborn foals do learn very quickly but how long this enhanced learning period lasts is unknown. Horse behaviorists do feel that foals have a tendency to go under dark objects and follow large moving objects right after birth. This hardwiring puts the foal in the right place to nurse (the dark underside of their mother) and gives it the tendency to follow its mother. Early in a foal's life, a mare will stop nursing and walk a short distance away. This action is thought to teach a foal to follow its mother. Certainly foals learn this very quickly as they seek the mother to continue their meal. Therefore, the argument of whether foals are imprintable becomes more of a semantic one. Whether you call it imprinting or a critical period, it does appear that foals have the ability to learn and assimilate large amounts of material within the first hours and days of life. The term imprinting has been the one popularized in several publications and therefore is the one that I am using here.

No matter which term you use, whether or not to imprint a foal remains controversial. I have found people that feel strongly on both sides. I personally have no problems with imprinting, assuming the foal is allowed to suckle and is not exhausted by an over-exuberant practitioner. There is certainly no evidence that practicing imprinting as it is published in Dr. Robert Miller's book *Imprint Training of the*

Newborn Foal is at all detrimental to the newborn foal.

Some preliminary studies have examined whether imprinted foals are more docile than foals that weren't imprinted but handled regularly. Handlers that were unaware of the foals' imprint status were unable to tell which foals had been imprinted. I cannot, however, comment on how the imprinting was done. Alternatively, I have found that proponents of imprinting feel strongly that foals that have been properly imprinted are easily identifiable as adults. I see many sick foals that require much care and handling after the first hours of life. These foals learn to tolerate being handled easily and without incident and have become habituated to many things as a result of their hospitalization even though the handling occurred after the first three hours of life. Some owners have told me that they think imprinted foals turned out to be sluggish and unresponsive adults. Others argue that imprinted foals make more trainable adults.

In the minutes following birth, it is important to make sure that the foal is strong, vigorous, and healthy. If he is not, contact your veterinarian immediately. It is also imperative that the mare and foal have some time together to bond and rest. It is important not just for the foal to bond with his mother but also for the mother to bond with the foal so that she does not reject it. This is especially true for mares having their first foal. Humans can be present during this time and may act as comfort and build confidence in a young nervous mare. Of course, both mare and foal should be examined to make sure they are safe and healthy. Foals will passively accept humans that are present during this time as well. The foal has several jobs to do during the first hours of life: breathe, bond with Mom, stand, and nurse. Colostrum is the first milk the mare produces, and it is rich in proteins and antibodies. Foals are born with few antibodies of their own to help fight off infection. Antibodies in Mom's colostrum help boost the foal's immune system, and the foal should receive colostrum soon after birth when the suckle reflex is present and strong. Because foals are particularly susceptible to infections, if you choose to imprint your foal make sure your hands and anything you put in the foal's mouth, around its head, or umbilicus is clean.

If you decide to imprint your foal, you may choose to do the imprinting before or after the foal has stood and suckled. Proponents of imprinting typically feel that soon after birth is better but certainly respect that colostrum intake is vital for the foal's health. Keep in mind that during this time the foal often struggles through the period of flooding until the procedure is complete and that foals are born with limited energy reserves. Therefore, you may choose to limit the number of items you habituate the foal to at this time and introduce others later so as not to exhaust the foal. For recommended procedures the reader is directed to *Imprint Training of the Newborn Foal*. Certainly, if you choose to imprint the foal, take the time to learn and study what you are about to do before undertaking the task.

My opinion is that you probably can habituate a foal just as thoroughly if you wait a few hours or until the next day and then continue to work with the foal on a daily basis. Certainly, proponents of imprinting may disagree and only time and additional scientific studies will tell for sure.

If you decide you want to use imprinting on your foal, you must remember the principles of habituation and flooding as a form of habituation as they apply to the practice of imprinting. First, recognize that you will likely have to expose the foal to the different objects or situations more than once to get the best result. Also, when exposing the foal to objects, you must expose him until he stops resisting, which is the basic tenet of flooding; otherwise, you may be inadvertently sensitizing him to that object. So again, if you choose to imprint the foal, be sure to study and understand the procedure thoroughly. You may desire to use additional controlled, multiple exposures over time either with or without previous imprinting to habituate your foal. An added bonus to continuing to work with your foal regularly is that your foal will learn to trust you in a way that may not happen from a single session of imprinting.

The question may be raised about whether an imprinted foal that is minimally handled in the days or weeks following imprinting would be as docile as a foal that was not imprinted yet handled daily. To my knowledge no controlled studies have examined this issue. Certainly, if you handle your foal daily you will be able to teach him many behaviors that could not be taught in a single imprinting session. In addition, by interacting with him daily you will know how healthy he is and you will be building trust. I certainly do not feel that imprinting is wrong. I just want owners to be aware that the mare and foal must bond, and that the foal must not be imprinted at the expense of time used to learn how to stand, walk, and nurse. And because imprinting is a type of flooding, owners need to understand that if imprinting is done improperly, they may be sensitizing the foal to the very stimuli that they are trying to desensitize him to. Therefore, they must study and be familiar with the technique before they undertake it.

5

Cues

We have talked about cues in two contexts thus far. First, we have used pressure (such as swinging a rope) as a cue and the removal of pressure as a negative reward. Second, we have introduced the use of oral cues to prompt behaviors we already have made strides in shaping, as in our orange cone example (see Chapter 3). In general, a cue can be added at any time during or after the development of a behavior. You may choose to teach a behavior with one cue and then replace it with another. This is accomplished using the new cue just before the established cue until the horse begins to perform the behavior when the new cue is given. The old cue then fades away and is not used anymore. In some instances it may be better to add a cue later in the process of teaching a behavior rather than earlier; this is done to avoid something called **learned irrelevance**.

Learned irrelevance

Learned irrelevance occurs when animals have learned to ignore a cue because there is no incentive for them to pay attention to it. That is the horse is either not rewarded for responding to the cue and so ignores it or the horse has heard the word or sound being used as the cue so many times that it lacks specific meaning. For example, say that today you have decided to teach your dog to come when called. Up until today you have routinely said things like "come" and "come here" when your dog was running around the yard and you wanted her to come to you. Her usual response has been to ignore you, which is why you have decided to teach her a specific cue that tells her she should come to you right away. You put the leash on her, say "come," and pull her toward you. When she gets to you, you give her lots of positive rewards. However, because she has heard you say "come" many times in her past and always ignored the word, she may be slower to realize that *now* the word "come" means something. She may actually learn this new skill faster if you use a different word such as "front." Her ignoring the word "come" is learned irrelevance. To

This horse is responsive to his rider's leg cues.

avoid learned irrelevance, you may choose to use novel words or actions as cues when teaching new behaviors.

Another example of learned irrelevance is a horse that is dull to the leg. We will assume that when the leg cue was originally taught, the horse responded to it by moving forward. However, since that time the horse has been ridden by a rider who repeatedly failed to remove leg pressure when the horse responded to it. The horse has been exposed to the cue many times yet has not been rewarded for responding. Therefore, he has learned to ignore the leg cue because there is no longer incentive for him to respond. Our goal is to apply cues consistently and remove them immediately as the horse responds in order to maintain our horse's sensitivity to them.

Types of cues

The cues we use with horses take many shapes and forms. Not only do we use oral cues, but we use our weight in the

The round pen is a good place for early lessons.

saddle, our legs, and hands. We also use tools such as whips and ropes to convey cues. Many times the cue you choose depends on the behavior you are teaching and where you are teaching it. That is, horses readily learn that there may be a different cue for a similar movement in different situations. For example, let us review teaching a young horse to canter.

First, the horse learned to move around the round pen when you swung a lead rope at him. Then you may have added the oral cue "canter" immediately before you swung the rope. Once the spoken cue was firmly established, you may have chosen to fade the rope twirl in favor of the oral cue. Now, you may move on to teach the horse to canter under saddle. You urge the horse forward with your seat and legs then use the spoken cue "canter" until he obeys. Because he knows the oral cue from his ground training, he should quickly generalize it to under-saddle work. As you urge your horse forward with your seat and legs, you are introducing

Here the horse learns to move away from the swinging rope.

your new cue. Soon the horse should start cantering with the leg or seat cue before you even say "canter." Then you can fade out the oral command and use the leg cue only. This involves many steps but typically does not cause anxiety by racing the horse into a canter. Overall the process goes more quickly than you might think.

A second method involves direct transfer of a groundwork cue to under-saddle work. If your horse has learned that a tap on the rump with a rope or dressage whip means canter, you may use the cue under saddle by tapping him on the rump with the free mecate rein or a dressage whip. You can then add a leg or seat cue to precede the tap on the rump until the horse has learned the new under-saddle cue and then fade out the tap on the rump. Both methods are effective and perfectly acceptable. You can decide which method to use to teach your horse different under-saddle skills.

Fading

The above example of teaching a young horse to canter demonstrates the use of fading, which occurs when you replace one cue with another. This is done by placing the new cue in front of the established cue. Through classical conditioning (see Chapter 3) the horse will start to respond to the new cue. Once the horse is responding to the new cue, the frequency and strength of the old cue can be diminished and then stopped altogether. We use fading to replace the coarse, obvious cues that we use to train younger horses with the subtle seat and hand cues that define the well-trained horse.

Cue intensity

How strongly a cue is applied is also important. I mean strength as in both harshness and in how obvious the cue is to the horse. For example, if you want to teach your horse to move forward from the touch of a whip, you might tap him lightly and repeatedly until he moves forward and then reward the forward movement. The annoyance of the constant light tapping makes the cue obvious to the horse and is usually enough to initiate movement. Because the tapping is rhythmical it is also obvious to him when you have stopped it. This accentuates your negative reward. Of course, you do not need to hit him very hard. As we have already discussed, your horse will likely interpret a forceful cue as punishment, and he may become fearful of the cue.

Exaggerated movement is another way to make a new cue obvious. For example, you may want to teach your horse to back up when you lean slightly back in the saddle. You will first teach him to back from the ground in response to a spoken cue, a rein cue, or both. Then you will have him generalize this cue to under-saddle work. In the beginning you will

The jockey's use of the whip is an obvious cue to the horse to move forward.

lean back fairly far just before you apply the backing cue. Soon he will associate backing with your shift in body weight and then you can fade out your original cues. Finally, you can decrease the intensity of the weight cue by leaning back slightly less with each lesson. Provided you continue to reward his behavior, he will eventually back with a minimal weight shift. The result will be a smooth transition into reverse without you pulling on your horse's mouth.

Horses that have learned to ignore a cue due to previous poor training may need cues to be applied more obviously than horses that are learning a new cue. For example, consider the horse that ignores the tap of a whip or the application of leg pressure to make him move forward while under saddle. He can be retrained using a simple method. Start by tapping lightly with a dressage or other whip behind the girth where you apply leg pressure and very gradually increase the strength and frequency of the taps. An alternative to this method is to tap with your legs. You may need to get pretty strong. At the same time make sure the horse has the freedom to move forward (you should not pull on his mouth). As soon as he moves forward, praise and reward him by stopping the tapping (negative reward) and perhaps offering a treat or a rub (positive reward). Repeat this procedure over and over. By slowly increasing the intensity of the cue each time, you will find that with each exercise he will respond sooner and to less pressure. Remember to reward his improvements. By repeating this exercise over several days you should be able to reform him. Your goal may be to show him the whip or just lay it against him and have him move forward. This procedure should be performed in a methodical and rhythmic way. If you loose your cool and beat your horse with the whip, you may end up with a sensitized horse that cannot work while his rider is even carrying a whip.

Because young horses have not learned to ignore many cues due to improper training and reinforcement, increasing the intensity of the pressure is rarely required. Instead, applying the cue in a rhythmic or steady fashion is often enough pressure to initiate movement.

Chaining

Chaining is a powerful training tool. It allows you to train complex behaviors in a very efficient way. Have you ever seen a dog in a show run out on stage, pick up an object, climb up a ladder, and put the object on a shelf? The trainer did not start by trying to teach the dog the entire sequence. Instead she broke the sequence down into a series of behaviors, taught each behavior in turn, and finally chained them together. One powerful way of chaining behaviors is to teach the final behavior first. This final behavior is followed by positive rewards. Then a new behavior is added in front of the final behavior. This new behavior is now rewarded by the

I push Reigna into the canter...

...then reward her for responding.

opportunity to perform the final behavior and get a reward. In this way, long chains of behaviors can be created.

Round penning is a perfect situation in which to teach behaviors by chaining. First, my horses learn that when I back up they may come to the center of the pen to get a rub and a break. This rewards them on several levels. First they get to rest, second they may get a treat, and third they get social interaction and rubbing from me. Now if I am teaching Reigna the canter departure, I may push her into a canter, and as soon as she canters I can click or say "good" (the secondary rewards I have taught my horses) and back up. She happily stops cantering and comes to me for a love and maybe a tidbit (intermittent reinforcement). Once this behavior is established, I can insist that she continue to canter even after I have rewarded the departure. Once she has cantered one or more times around the pen, I can then back up to invite her in. Therefore, I am rewarding her continued time cantering by offering her the opportunity to perform the final behavior in the chain, which is initiated by my backing up and inviting her to come to the center of the pen. By adding behaviors slowly, I can chain inside and outside turns, upward and downward transitions, and other movements together, all ending with the opportunity to come into the center for a rest and a scratch. I can reward each response with my secondary reinforcer, as well as removing pressure to reward individual behaviors. Then I ultimately reward her by inviting her to the center for lots of positive rewards, including rest.

Chained behaviors can always be the same, such as the dog going across the stage and up the ladder, or different each time, as when I work Reigna or Tieler in the round pen. I do not ask them for the same sequence of actions each time we work in the pen but ask them to work for various periods doing different behaviors and then reward them with the opportunity to come into the middle.

Searching

I am sure that searching is not unique to the horse, but it is fascinating to watch the process of searching in horses once you recognize it. Searching occurs when the horse explores his various options to determine which choice is the one that will be met with reward. One example of searching takes place when you watch a horse that is being taught to enter a horse trailer. The horse does not want to go into the trailer so he tries moving to the left, then moving to the right, then backward, sometimes up, and then, finally forward. This is assuming that he is unsuccessful in avoiding the trailer when going in any other direction besides forward. If he is successful in avoiding going forward, then he will repeatedly go in that successful direction until that avenue is closed to him. Therefore, you can see that we run

***A horse exhibiting searching behavior while learning
to load into a trailer.***

into problems most often when training a horse to enter a
trailer and he gets away with going in any direction other
than forward.

An interesting example of searching occurred when I first
taught Reigna to jump. She had gone over ground rails many
times and I had introduced her to small cross-rails. After pop-
ping over the cross-rail several times one day she decided to
explore her options. She stopped at the cross-rail and tried to
go right. I responded by using the rein and my leg to keep her
facing the jump. Then she tried to go left, and I corrected her
the same way. The jump was small, and so if she stepped over
it I was going to be happy with the response. To my great surprise she dropped to her knees for a split second. She prompt-
ly stood up and then stepped over the jump. It was very funny.
I am not sure if she was toying with the idea of going under
the jump or lying down. I am happy she decided both were
poor options. We continued with positive rewards for going

over the jump, and I have not had a similar problem since.

Horses start searching as soon as you begin training them. It is natural for them to try to understand what is being asked. So it is appropriate to let a horse search without punishing him for it. If you are pressing your horse to go around the round pen and you want him to turn to face you, you may find him performing other maneuvers such as reversing direction, slowing down, or going faster. If these activities go unrewarded, it is likely that he will eventually look to you for leadership, which is a behavior that you can reinforce through positive and negative rewards. However, if you punish him for trying each of these alternative behaviors, you may end up evoking the fight or flight response. He may try to leave the round pen by going over it or through it. His other option is to stop trying. Both are bad options; in the first he may injure himself, and in the second he may be hurt emotionally. If you discourage the horse from searching, he may stop trying. If your horse refuses to search, it will make teaching him any behavior very difficult. In addition, excessive punishment will cause your horse to fear and not respect you. If your horse respects you, he will look to you for leadership and will search in an attempt to determine what you want from him.

This is similar to a family situation that can develop when a child gets heavily criticized for how he or she performs when participating in hobbies or sports. If Mom or Dad constantly corrects or criticizes the child, pretty soon the child will stop engaging in any extracurricular activities to avoid constant criticism. If we want to encourage a horse, we have to do it by providing excellent leadership. Horses naturally challenge their leaders in an effort to ensure that only the best horses guide the herd. By channeling our horse's direction of movement in the round pen, barn, or while under saddle, we are establishing our dominant position within the herd. Our leadership role is strengthened when we reaffirm our horse's trust by rewarding desired behaviors and avoiding excessive punishment.

Examples of cues and chaining

In the picture below I am backing up. Reigna is looking at me and starting to turn toward the center of the arena. This usually follows a string or chain of well-executed behaviors. For example, I had sent her to the outside of the pen and asked her to walk, trot, and canter. As a reward for performing these behaviors I am allowing her to perform this final one, which she knows well, where I back up and she can come to me in the center of the arena and rest. I may also choose to reward her with a treat (intermittent reinforcement). Therefore, she has learned that when working in the round pen she will ultimately be rewarded by the opportunity to perform this final behavior: turning into the center,

I back away to reward Reigna.

Tieler responds to my request to bend.

stopping, resting, and getting a treat and a rub from me.

Above you see me applying some subtle cues to teach Tieler obedience and flexibility. In this photo I have cued him with the lead rope to turn his haunches away Removal of the cue is being used as a negative reward. The pressure applied on the rope will be released as he complies. I will also use primary rewards to reinforce the behaviors.

Appendix

Final Thoughts

S ince I consider myself an educator rather than a horse trainer, I would like you, as a student, to consider this: after reading this book, *how would you...*

• stop a horse from shying in the same place in the arena, such as a corner or a door?
  • teach a horse to tie?
  • get a horse to cross a creek?
  • accustom a horse to electric clippers?
  • catch a horse in a field?
  • get a horse to load into a trailer?
• stop your horse from invading your personal space and walking over you?

Here is a checklist of questions you can ask yourself to help figure out the answers.

• What exactly is my horse doing that is incorrect?
• Is this problem a manifestation of a larger problem that must be addressed? What are other symptoms that may be part of this larger problem?

• What are the different methods I have at my disposal to approach correcting this problem?

• Do I have the mental knowledge and physical ability to implement the plan I have in mind to correct this problem? That is, can I do this safely and effectively?

• Do I want to tackle this at all or do I want to have a professional attempt to fix this?

• If I am going to do this on my own, where in this process will I need a helping hand? (For example, a person on the ground to be an objective observer to give you feedback that you are doing what you think you are doing). Who is my resource? Is he or she well trained and capable?

• After implementing your plan, you will need to assess your progress. Have you really fixed the problem or simply applied a quick fix patch that may not correct the problem long term? What do you need to do to fix this problem long term?

Horse owners frequently ask me questions about changing specific behaviors. For example, "How do I keep my horse from biting me? He does it every time I go to put on his bridle."

I can give them some ideas on how to punish the horse for biting, but then I am not addressing the bigger and more important issue: why is the horse biting in the first place. Such a horse-owner pair likely has larger dominance issues and the symptom of the disease is that the horse bites. Therefore, it is important to remember that fixing the symptom does not cure the disease.

Once you have defined your problem, think about what other behaviors your horse is exhibiting that might also be a consequence of this problem. You will need to include these behaviors in your plan to reform you and your horse as well.

Now you start to formulate your plan. After reading this book and others and by taking riding lessons you may feel that you have a pretty good knowledge base from which to make a plan. Will you use punishments? Negative rewards? Positive rewards? Will you use treats to teach your horse not to bite? Of course not.

Make sure your plan makes sense. And don't hesitate to ask a professional trainer for help when necessary. Either have your trainer help you fix the problem by working together or have your trainer deal with it first and then include you in the loop.

By approaching problems with your horse objectively and using available resources, it is my hope that you will have a lifelong, positive relationship with your horse.

Photo Credits

Chapter 1: Anne M. Eberhardt, 14, 16.

Chapter 2: Anne M. Eberhardt, 22; CLiX Photography, 26; Cheryl Manista, 27.

Chapter 3: Anne M. Eberhardt, 35; John Sorrenti, 48, 50, 55, 62, 68, 69, 72-74.

Chapter 4: Anne M. Eberhardt, 79, 81; Cheryl Manista, 84.

Chapter 5: *The Horse* magazine; Anne M. Eberhardt, 91, 92; Benoit & Associates, 94; John Sorrenti, 96, 97, 101, 102.

Cover photo: Anne M. Eberhardt
Back cover photo: John Sorrenti

About the Author

Dr. Jennifer MacLeay is a graduate of the University of New Hampshire and attended veterinary school at The Ohio State University College of Veterinary Medicine. She then practiced in Charlottesville, Virginia, before completing a residency and doctorate program in large animal internal medicine at the University of Minnesota. Dr. MacLeay is board certified by the American College of Veterinary Internal Medicine and practices and teaches at Colorado State University's College of Veterinary Medicine as an Assistant Professor.

Her interest in horses began with hunt seat equitation and then expanded to include dressage and eventing. She currently enjoys all forms of equitation and natural horsemanship.

Dr. MacLeay, her husband, three horses, three dogs, and two cats live in northern Colorado.